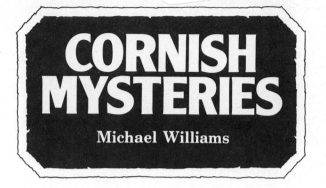

CORNISH MYSTERIES

Michael Williams

BOSSINEY BOOKS

First published in 1980
by Bossiney Books
St Teath, Bodmin, Cornwall
Designed, Typeset and printed in Great Britain by
Penwell Ltd., Parkwood, Callington
Cornwall

ISBN 0 906456 45 2

PLATE ACKNOWLEDGMENTS

Cover photograph by David Golby
Page 5 David & Joan Wills
Pages 19, 29 Kerry Mudd
Pages 11, 12 Richard Hawken
Pages 37, 67 John Chard
Pages 54, 57, 82 A. Lennox-Boyd
Page 40 Woolf-Greenham Collection
Page 72 by courtesy of Spencer Thorn
Pages 7-9, 21, 30, 32, 39, 41-51, 63, 64, 69, 87, 92 Ray Bishop
Page 76 Southgate Studios
Page 23 Grindley Studios
Page 61 Osborne Studios
Page 91 David Halfyard
Page 25 David Clarke
Page 74 Joan Rendell
Page 60 Piran Bishop
Page 66 John Watts
Page 38 David Mudd
Page 31 Murray King

ABOUT THE AUTHOR

A Cornishman, Michael Williams started full time publishing in 1975. With his wife Sonia, he runs Bossiney Books from a cottage and converted barn in North Cornwall — they are literally Cornish cottage publishers, specializing in Westcountry subjects by Westcountry authors.

For ten years they ran the Bossiney House Hotel, just outside Tintagel — hence the name Bossiney Books. Then in 1975 they left the hotel business and moved to St Teath. This is their sixty-first title.

The author of nine books, Michael Williams says: 'I enjoy this way of life immensely, publishing full-time and promoting the work of our writers, and still managing to find time to do a book of my own now and then. It's hard work, very challenging but very fulfilling.'

Cornish Mysteries, he explains, 'is a kind of jig-saw puzzle in words and pictures . . . though you'll find pieces are still missing, and that adds to the fascination. The truth is nobody knows the final answer to most of these stories. They are quite simply mysteries.

Cornish Mysteries

I am usually bad about dates, but Midsummer Eve 1965 stands out with diamond sharpness.

That night, around midnight I experienced something that defied any logical or satisfactory human explanation. Of course, I didn't know it at the time but those mysterious lights appearing inside the chapel at Bossiney were to have a profound influence. They instantly killed all cynicism, and were eventually to open doors — and windows. Without them, I would not be writing this book — and you would not be reading these words. Without them, Sonia and I would not now be running a publishing business from a Cornish cottage.

Looking back to that Midsummer Eve, I now see those lights and that shared experience probably had as much effect on me as many of the splendid sermons heard years ago in Nonconformist chapels. They proved to be a natural springboard for a whole new approach to an important aspect of Life. From that night onward, conversations about extraordinary things became natural — ordinary in fact. The Doubting Thomas died that summer's evening, and as a result of his death a new sympathy was born, whereby people could talk to me about *their* experiences without fear of ridicule.

As a result of that Midsummer Eve experience, I began researching into claims of genuine Supernatural experience in the county. The sculptor and author Sven Berlin told me: 'You have chosen a rich mine to reopen.' Fascinating accounts came in from all over Cornwall, and *Supernatural in Cornwall* was the result: a book that helped to firmly establish Bossiney as Cornish publishers. But I realised by geographically restricting the accounts I had lost some good Devon stories. So *Occult in the West*, coming in its wake and incorporating Devonshire experiences, was an inevitable successor.

This book, following first *Supernatural in Cornwall* and then *Occult in the West,* means that I have interviewed nearly one hundred and fifty people, claiming ghostly sightings or unusual experiences. Interestingly they have come from contrasting sections of society. A Canon of the Church of England, an author, a former High Sheriff of Cornwall, a housewife, a retired Army Officer, a hotelier — these are only a handful of many who have seen things that have defied logical explanation — and it has been difficult to find a common denominator. Though the majority did have blue eyes! So there is almost certainly something in that ancient Romany belief that blue is the most spiritual of all colours. Furthermore all the men and women have convinced me of their sincerity. In all three books facts have been my aim. Where and when doubt lurked in my mind — and sometimes inconsistency or inaccuracy did emerge — then events never advanced beyond my

**'Sven Berlin told me "You have chosen a rich mine to reopen."
Fascinating accounts came in from all over Cornwall.'**

notebook. Many of the accounts that did convince me, were because they were undramatic — very matter of fact — some perhaps even a little lightweight. Then why 'invent' that kind of experience?

Anyway as I was writing *Occult's* Postscript, I knew that a third book was waiting to be written: *Cornish Mysteries*. Sven Berlin was very right. It is a rich mine.

There is though one important difference, these mysteries are not exclusively Supernatural in nature. Some of the episodes are very down-to-earth, very much of this world. But the thread running through them is a mysterious 'something'. Once more, there has been the problem of that final full stop — the brutal truth is nobody knows the answer or solution to many of these stories.

But is that surprising? After all, Cornwall is not only a beautiful and mysterious landscape, it is peppered with puzzles and unanswered questions.

Cornwall has been called the Land of Saints and Sinners: perfectly true but it is also the country of the superstitious. This strain of superstition ran through our traditional industries of mining and fishing in that miners and fishermen were not permitted to whistle when on duty. And it's no use my pretending that I'm immune: either meeting people on a staircase or walking under a ladder can cast a shadow on the brightest day. I love wandering around churchyards, but you'll find me treading carefully. Perhaps Coleridge's words are a warning:

> *To see a man tread over graves,*
> *I hold it no good mark;*
> *'Tis wicked in the sun and moon*
> *And bad luck in the dark!*

The Cornish atmosphere, of course, works on different people in differing degrees. A reader of *Supernatural* and *Occult*, writing from her home in Kent, said: 'Some years ago we were staying at Five Lanes and went to Boscastle for the evening. On the way to Boscastle we noticed a reservoir amongst the trees, and we drew off the road to look at it but I felt evil at that place. I felt as if something was either going to pull me into the water or push me in. To make matters worse, we lost our way in the mist on the journey back and ended up right at this dreadful place. I felt as if we were being pulled there . . . I was almost hysterical.'

So that strange 'something' that sent Walter de la Mare fleeing

'Cornwall is not only a beautiful and mysterious landscape, it is peppered with puzzles and unanswered questions.'

from Cornwall all those years ago is still here — for some people anyway.

The novelist may think himself to be a superior character of creativity — and I believe he generally is, but these three excursions have taught me that fact can be stronger, stranger and more fascinating than fiction.

May I quote just one example in the shaping of this publication. Five years ago, in the early days of full-time Bossiney publishing, I hit upon the idea of a book composed of a dozen profiles of famous eccentrics. The manuscript chapters came in, one by one, many of them excellent, but I realised eventually it was the kind of book that

'I love wandering around churchyards, but you'll find me treading carefully . . .'

needed hardcovers and a national distribution — something beyond our resources as cottage paperback publishers. I tried to interest two national publishing houses — they gave the idea serious consideration but ultimately said 'No'. It was clearly a case of falling between two areas of publishing. I was bitterly disappointed and found it a difficult job, writing letters to a dozen contributors, returning their manuscripts.

One essay, that I found particularly hurtful to return, was to Laura Farnworth at Warleggan Rectory. Initially I had planned to write the chapter on Densham, the hermit-like Rector of Warleggan, but on visiting Laura and Roger Farnworth at the old Rectory, I quickly discovered she was not only a writer but had a lot of original material on the last resident Rector. I immediately suggested she should be the author, and offered some background information I had obtained from old files of *The Cornish Guardian*.

In a telephone conversation with Laura Farnworth, something like three years ago, I expressed the sincere hope that her work on Densham might still see the light of publication day. Then, one

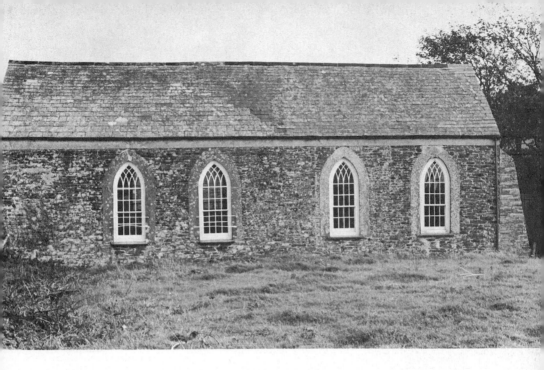

'. . . those lights . . . inside the chapel at Bossiney were to have a profound influence.'

morning on BBC's Morning SouWest, we heard the shattering news: she had died the previous day in a drowning accident in the Channel Islands — a tragic and early death.

As *Cornish Mysteries* began to grow — in a curious fashion some books almost write themselves in that ideas suddenly take shape — and this was a case — I instinctively felt Densham should be included because his whole life in Cornwall was a mystery. Moreover I knew Laura Farnworth, in that manuscript, had pinned him to paper with great authority and clarity. In a quite uncanny way, she *knew* the man.

So I thought what better method of resurrecting her work than using it inside these pages. Her husband Roger readily agreed, and apart from cutting the odd sentence here and there, it is essentially her voice, her work. One sunlit Saturday morning I sat, once more, inside the old Rectory and re-read her manuscript chapter, five years on, and realised that it *could* have been written for this book, Laura's last sentence fitting the title and overall theme like a glove.

Stranger than fiction indeed.

The Ann Hearn Murder Trial

Murder is often a mystery.

What drives a man or woman to kill is sometimes shrouded like the ultimate corpse — or like the Cornish landscape on a misty morning. Certainly in the annals of crime in Cornwall Mrs Sarah Ann Hearn emerges as one of the most mysterious, most baffling characters of all.

Back in the 1920s Mrs Hearn shared a house in North Cornwall with her invalid sister Mrs Everard. They lived at Trenhorne House, Lewannick. In July 1930 Mrs Everard died, and thereafter Ann Hearn became increasingly friendly with her neighbours, next door, Mr and Mrs William Thomas of Trenhorne Farm. The trio enjoyed outings and picnics, and one such excursion was to Bude in the October of that year. In a Bude cafe, they ordered some food *and* ate some salmon sandwiches made by Mrs Hearn back at Trenhorne. Later that day, Alice Thomas became ill: food poisoning being suspected. Her condition declined to such an extent that she was taken to a Plymouth hospital. But she never came home. She died on the fourth day of November, and the subsequent post-mortem revealed white arsenic in her body.

Ann Hearn attended her neighbour's funeral, but soon after vanished. She did though leave a note for William Thomas. 'I am innocent, innocent,' wrote Mrs Hearn, 'but she is dead, and it was my lunch she ate. I cannot stay. When I am dead they will be sure I am guilty, and you at least will be clear . . . My conscience is clear. I am not afraid of afterwards.'

A suicide note? It looked so when Ann Hearn's coat was found on the cliffs at Looe and one of her shoes was washed up on the beach. But the Police were not convinced.

Moreover their doubts were justified, for Ann Hearn was discovered in Torquay working as a housekeeper under the quaintly

Trenhorne Farm, the home of Mr and Mrs William Thomas.

Ann Hearn's home, Trenhorne House, near Lewannick.

'I have stood in front of that severe granite-faced building at the Bodmin Assizes and wondered.'

assumed name of 'Mrs Faithful'. She was arrested and charged with the murders of Mrs Thomas and Mrs Everard. Mrs Everard's grave, opened at Lewannick, revealed that she too had arsenic in her body. And if that were not enough to set tongues wagging, an aunt of Mrs Hearn and Mrs Everard buried in the same graveyard also had traces of arsenic in her body!

I have wandered among those graves in North Cornwall, have visited Trenhorne Farm and looked across to Ann Hearn's old home next door. I have stood in front of that severe granite-faced building at the Bodmin Assizes — and wondered. Has Cornish crime known a more astonishing case? I doubt it. Even today the whole thing has an air of Agatha Christie fiction. Weedkiller planted in the sandwiches?

In June 1931 Ann Hearn faced a double murder charge at Bodmin. While village gossip accused her of wanting to marry William Thomas.

It was a strange twist of irony that brought Ann Hearn back to Cornwall to face this charge. Her Torquay employer, Mr Cecil Parker, had followed the Hearn case with interest, and recognised her photograph in a newspaper report — and promptly lost his appetite! Anyway Cecil Parker reported her to the Police and having collected the five hundred pound reward, he generously handed it over as a contribution towards the cost of her defence. So Mrs Hearn was able to acquire the services of the most brilliant defence lawyer in the land.

The smart middle-aged woman denied all three allegations. Her only admission was that courage deserted her at Looe when she had contemplated suicide. The case itself turned into a classic battle between two men: Mr du Parq for the prosecution and Mr Norman Birkett, later Lord Birkett, for the defence. The seventh day brought high drama and the turning point in the whole case. Mr du Parq had been summing up for nearly half-an-hour when his face flushed crimson and then went a deathly white. He swayed, fell back into the arms of a clerk and was carried out of court.

What efffect did this have on the jury?

Nearly half-a-century on, we can only guess. But in the words of one member of the jury it were 'as if the Almighty had struck down the man who sought to prosecute an innocent woman'.

David Mudd, in a brilliant reconstruction of the case, in the concluding chapter of *Facets of Crime*, recalled Mr Birkett's powerful closing speech for the defence.

'For almost four hours Mr Birkett sifted and re-sifted the evidence. Showing remarkable forensic knowledge, he discredited the Prosecution's allegations of deliberate poisoning. With an impeccable sense of occasion, he spoke of "the dramatic happenings in the peaceful village of Lewannick".

'Sometimes his voice rang loud and powerful through the court; sometimes it dropped to a mere whisper. With beautiful prose, he spoke passages of pathos; with a fencer's sudden thrust he threw forward a vital point towards the jury.

'The Crown's case, he said, depended on all sorts of coincidences and rare possibilities. The "motive" that Mrs Hearn had killed Mrs Thomas to enable her to marry the widower was, Mr Birkett said, "fantastical, fanciful and absurd". There was no evidence to substantiate the claim.

'A major Prosecution technical witness had spoken of the effects of arsenic poisoning, yet had admitted that he had never treated a living person suffering from it. "Yet he speaks of symptoms with the same confidence that he spoke of other matters," Mr Birkett observed tartly before rejecting the evidence with the curt: "Let the cobbler stick to his last."

'Dealing with the churchyard exhumation of the body of Mrs Everard, he again recalled the admission of another Crown witness that it was possible that arsenic-impregnated dust particles had either blown on to the body during the autopsy; had somehow entered the unsealed specimen jar; or else that arsenic from the soil had seeped its way into the coffin and been absorbed by the body.

'He recalled that the witness had agreed that the arsenic traces were so minute that even the slightest error in calculation would make a material and vital difference. He suggested that there was no evidence that Mrs Hearn had administered arsenic to any person or in any form.

'He reminded the jury of evidence that at Trenhorne Farm there were some worm tablets that contained not only arsenic, but also copper which the weedkiller did not contain. He pointed out that the post-mortem examination of Mrs Thomas had found traces of copper as well as arsenic.

'Dealing with the trip to Bude and the sandwiches, Mr Birkett pointed out that they were placed on the table in two piles each of three sandwiches. Nobody had handed Mrs Thomas any one particular sandwich, and Mr and Mrs Thomas and Mrs Hearn had all picked at random from the pile.

'Indeed, Mr Birkett recalled, there might well be in the jury's mind recollection of the evidence that if there was poison, and if the poison was of the type suggested by the Crown, then the sandwiches would have been noticeably discoloured.

'The death of Mrs Thomas, he suggested, could not be directly attributable to Mrs Hearn. He submitted that the initial reason for Mrs Thomas's illness after the trip to Bude was ordinary food poisoning occasioned by the tinned salmon in the sandwiches. Although she died seventeen days later in hospital in Plymouth, Mrs Hearn could not have been responsible, he claimed.

'Dealing with the character of Mrs Hearn, Mr Birkett drew a work portrait of a quiet, sincere woman. He spoke of the straightforward way in which she had answered questions. Referring to the "suicide" note, he suggested to the jury that it was consistent with the actions of a woman very upset, very grieved, and very distraught, who meant "to take her life if she could screw up her courage to the sticking point". Her anguish had been caused by local allegations and suspicions in Lewannick that she had killed Mrs Thomas.

'Mr Birkett later said that he entered the court with the intention of basing his final address to the jury on some words in the Gospel according to St John.

'Recalling that one of the witnesses had spoken of Mrs Hearn reading Bible passages to the ailing Mrs Everard, Mr Birkett had decided to open his address with the words: "Let not your heart be troubled, neither let it be afraid."

'However, against the drama of the morning and the very obvious effect that Mr du Parcq's seizure had had on the court, Mr Birkett changed his strategy.

'For the duration of the trial the weather had been dull with unbroken clouds and misty rain. Now, as he rose to his feet, the sun broke through and sent the first shafts of bright light dancing on the drab walls of the Assize Court.

'Without drawing attention to this "omen" in any obvious way, he concluded his four-hour address in these words:

"For over five months Mrs Hearn has lain in Exeter gaol. The darkness of the winter has now turned to the lovely light of this June day. For her, upon trial for her life, it may be said with truth she has been walking in the valley of great shadows. It is your hand and your hand alone which can lead her forth into the light. It is your voice and your voice alone that can speak to her the word of deliverance. My appeal is that you will speak that word, that you will stretch forth the hand. Your verdict ought to be and should be that she is not guilty. For that verdict I appeal."

His speech over, Mr Birkett, wet with perspiration from nervous tension, turned to Dingle Foot, his junior counsel, and said, '. . . cases like this take years off a man's life.' 'Perhaps,' replied Mr Foot, 'but they add years to the client's.'

We can well imagine what the media would have made of all of it today. We would be insensitive too if we would not, in our imagination, feel the agony of Mrs Hearn that night.

The next day, Mr Justice Roche did his summing-up — and it was no brief affair, lasting until three pm, when the jury trooped out to consider their verdict.

As the jury left the court, Mrs Hearn, for the first time in these eight gruelling days, broke down.

Mr Birkett, for his part, left Bodmin while the jury was still considering its verdict. Did he consider it a hopeless case? The official reason was that he had to be in London the next day for a High Court action. Anyway the remainder of the case he now left in the hands of Mr Dingle Foot.

The next hour must have been the longest in Mrs Hearn's life. The jury took exactly sixty minutes to reach their verdict.

'How do you find the prisoner?' asked Mr Justice Roche.

'Not guilty,' came the reply.

Women in the court cried. The nurse, alongside Mrs Hearn nearly passed out.

'Sarah Ann Hearn, you are discharged.'

That single sentence, from the lips of Mr Justice Roche, ended a sensational case — and Mrs Hearn walked from the court a free woman.

But in the eyes of many members of the public she was 'Guilty'. A small personal hint of public feeling had been shown at Pencrebar, the home of Mr Isaac Foot, the distinguished Westcountry lawyer, Liberal and Methodist. Mr Birkett, having been asked to plant a tree at Pencrebar, enquired from the gardener there, Mr Bennett, whether there was much arsenic in the soil. 'No more than there is in Lewannick Churchyard!' came the tart reply.

And the incredible story of this double murder doesn't end there. Outside and beyond the verdict, the deaths of Mrs Thomas and Mrs Everard remain total mysteries. Nobody has ever suggested that either woman committed suicide or died through accidently consuming a quantity of poison. So those two graves remain riddles in this unfinished jig-saw puzzle of crime.

And what of Sarah Ann Hearn?

She simply vanished. She was never seen again after that last day of the trial.

Indeed she made a cunning exit from the Assize Hall, that afternoon at Bodmin, by exchanging hats and coats with her other sister, a Mrs Poskitt from Yorkshire. The supposition was that she planned to go North with her sister, but from Bodmin she travelled to Launceston, where she had a meal at the King's Arms — and after that meal her life story remains an incredible blank.

I have walked along the deserted beach at Looe on a winter's morning, and wondered if she did finally commit suicide, this time leaving no note. Or did she take another assumed name and perhaps change her appearance. A wig perhaps?

As I said, Ann Hearn was one of the most mysterious, most baffling characters of all. Or am I wrong to use the past tense.

Is she still alive today? It's just possible.

Dreams

For as long as I can remember dreams have fascinated — and infuriated me. The trouble is I can remember only a fraction, and yet on waking I *know* I have just dreamt.

Some dreams, of course, have shaped the face of history. Three hundred years before the birth of Christ, Alexander the Great conquered the city of Tyre in Phoenicia, after dreaming the city was his. A form of clairvoyancy or a case of our thoughts being the ancestors of our deeds? We are told too that, roughly a hundred years later, Hannibal was inspired by dreams to make his historic march across the Alps with a train of elephants.

Religion and dreams are sometimes closely related. Back in the thirteenth century St Francis of Assisi found his road to religious awareness — and vocation — through dreams. Both Old and New Testaments in the Bible contain important references to dreams, and down the ages people have looked for guidance in their dream life.

One of the most remarkable dreams in British history occurred here in Cornwall — at Scorrier House, near Redruth. It was experienced by John Williams who had a nightmare quality dream not once but three times on three successive nights. Moreover each night he dreamed the same dream.

On the first day of May, 1812, he told friends and relations about this recurring dream. Nobody was in any doubt about the location of the dream experience: it was not Cornwall, it was, in vivid detail, the lobby inside the House of Commons. John Williams told the experience in such detail that nobody could fault him. He 'saw' very

'Suddenly John Bellingham . . . appeared from behind a pillar, raised his pistol and fired at the Prime Minister.' ▶

clearly someone, in a snuff-coloured coat with yellow metal buttons, drawing a pistol and killing a man wearing a blue coat with a white waistcoat.

He thought it might be wise to warn the authorities, but his wife and friends advised him not to do so. They argued it was only a dream and influential people in London might make him a laughing stock. Furthermore none of them could identify either the man with the pistol or the threatened man in the blue coat. It all sounded very sensible advice, so John Williams stayed in Cornwall — and otherwise silent.

What he and his wife and friends did not know was that, at this time, in London was an embittered man, John Bellingham by name. Bellingham had had some very nasty experiences in Russia where the Tzarist Police had arrested him, where he had been imprisoned and had lost both money and business. Bellingham was very bitter about it all. So much so that he had complained to the British Ambassador and the Consul-General, and when he returned to London he contacted numerous people, including the Prime Minister, about possible redress. But he had gained no satisfaction. 'You broke Russian law and the Government cannot intervene' — that was the reaction. All of which explained why Bellingham was lurking in the lobby of the House of Commons on the afternoon of the 11 May 1812.

Spencer Perceval, the Prime Minister, that afternoon too was under sharp attack and there were protests about the Prime Minister not being in the House to hear and answer the criticisms. Feelings ran so high that a message was sent to Downing Street and eventually the Prime Minister, 'a thin, pale and short man in a blue coat and white waistcoat, walked through the lobby of the House of Commons to the Chamber to hear the criticisms against him'.

Suddenly John Bellingham, wearing a snuff-coloured coat with yellow metal buttons, appeared from behind a pillar, raised his pistol and fired at the Prime Minister from point blank range. Spencer Perceval died in the Speaker's Chambers before the doctor arrived. Bellingham was promptly arrested and bundled into the cells of the Palace of Westminster.

Bellingham being an old Irish settler's name immediately fired

'The murderers were subsequently hanged at Bodmin Gaol.' ▶

the Parliamentary imagination and there were thoughts of a conspiracy. But Bellingham demolished that theory. 'It's a private injury. I know what I have done. It was a denial of justice on the part of the Government.' Thus Spencer Perceval, at the age of 49, became the only British Prime Minister to be murdered — or assassinated.

And history didn't end there: lawyers, anxious to have criminal insanity defined, referred the case to the Old Bailey. Bellingham's plea of insanity however was set aside — and he was sentenced to be hanged.

The speed and sequence of events were astonishing by present-day standards. The killing took place on 11th May, the Old Bailey trial ended on the 15th May and Bellingham was hanged on the 18th.

Recently walking around Egloshayle Churchyard at Wadebridge, I was reminded of another remarkable dream in Cornish history.

Here in this Churchyard you can find the grave of one Nevell Norway — an ancestor of the famous novelist Nevil Shute. He was murdered not far up the road by the Lightfoot brothers, James and William, on his way home from Bodmin Market in February 1840. It was a crime that aroused an enormous public sympathy. Details on the grey headstone show that over £3,000 — a sizeable sum of money in those days — was raised for his widow and six children.

This crime — and a mass of other interesting stories — are to be found inside the pages of Sabine Baring-Gould's *Cornish Characters and Strange Events* which was published back in 1908. Astonishingly, this murder was to have a Supernatural postscript, concerning Edmund Norway, brother of the murder victim. That very night, aboard a merchant ship bound for Cadiz, Edmund dreamt with appalling accuracy.

So vivid was the dream that Edmund, on waking, wrote about it, incredibly giving a number of *facts* about his brother's murder. At their trial the Lightfoot brothers confessed they had twice shot at Norway, and twice the pistol had failed to function. They had then struck him from the saddle and with several savage blows had killed him — all of which Edmund had 'seen' in his dream. The murderers were subsequently hanged at Bodmin Gaol, when a large crowd of

Acora, the Romany clairvoyant, with author, Colin Wilson. ▶

spectators travelled by a special railway excursion from Wadebridge.

In the light of that visit to Wadebridge, I talked to a man who treats dreams very seriously. Acora, the Westcountry's leading clairvoyant, lives with his wife Jeannette and young daughter Sammie Rebecca near Gunnislake overlooking the Tamar Valley. A Scorpio subject, Acora comes from a long line of travelling folk — he is a great grandson of the celebrated fortune-teller, Madame Zambra, whose clients included Royalty.

'I dream every night of my life,' he explained. 'We Romanies have long believed in the destiny of dreams. Even the Bible contains a prophetic dream concerning cattle. That famous dream, in Genesis, is believed to have saved Egypt from a terrible famine.

'Only a fool would ignore his dream life. Dreams can carry a message from the subconscious — and we would be wise to heed those messages, for dreams can tell us a lot about ourselves; they can reveal our fears and emotions — and can release hidden tensions.

'Much though depends on the ability to interpret dreams. To remember a dream is not enough. The key to it all lies in an accurate interpretation, and, over the years, through my Romany ancestry and my work in the clairvoyant field, I have built up a kind of Dream Dictionary.

'Did you know, for example, that dreams often work in reverse?

'Let's say you dream of a wedding. Well, that could mean a funeral. Or if you dream of good fortune this often forecasts some kind of punishment or suffering. Or dreaming of a dead body doesn't necessarily mean death; it could indicate finding treasure or money coming to you unexpectedly.

'Some dreams are meant as warnings — as I give people the gypsy's warning when my clairvoyancy picks up something dark in their future. Nightmares though are always ominous, and recurring nightmares would almost certainly mean the need to consult a doctor — or specialist in matters of the mind.

'I find absence an interesting dream. When I dream of someone I've not seen for a long time, the odds are that person will soon reappear in my life, their appearance in the dream experience then has a clairvoyant quality.

'Here are some dream examples and our Romany interpretation of them: seeing an actress performing on stage in a play; that means bad luck; if you're talking to her it means success; if you make love to her that means joy will be yours; but if you take her out for dinner or to a party that means bad luck.

'Apples too can mean different things. If you're taking apples from a tree, this could mean persecution. But if you're eating ripe apples, the indications are that you're destined for happiness; whereas if the apples are sour there's likely to be a quarrel.

'A bath also has various interpretations; as do breasts. Clear water in a bath signifies good health; dirty water forecasts death; a large breast suggests good fortune; while dreaming of small breasts predicts failure.

'Clouds in a dream depend on the shade: black clouds spell misfortune; white clouds happiness.'

Our conversation then moved from the sky to the animal kingdom, for Acora is quite convinced that the 'seeing of animals in our dreams can tell us something too about things to come.

'Dogs are interesting dream subjects,' he said, 'because they

'Dogs are interesting dream subjects . . .'

mean so many different things.

'The vision of a dog usually means all friends will be true. If a dog sleeps, good luck. If he barks, keep quiet and if he runs behind you, there could be slander. A dog fighting a cat means quarrels; and dog v. dog represents persecution.

'Cats, on the whole, are bad dreams, for they represent treachery or disappointment — and loss.

'Faces too mean different things: when a man dreams of a beautiful woman, pleasure and happiness will be his; but an ugly face means evil. Whereas when a woman dreams of a good-looking man, she will soon marry. Eyes equally have a variety of meanings: pretty eyes, happiness. Dull eyes, faults that irritate. Loving eyes, deceit. Eyes closed, an unfaithful mistress. Loss of eyesight, a jealous wife.

'Some things have a surprising interpretation. For instance if you quarrel in a dream, it predicts a swift marriage. Now rags generally would suggest poverty and a down-and-out life. Yet if you're wearing rags in a dream, prosperity will be yours.

'These then are only some of hundreds of dream interpretations. Dream symbols may seem fantastic, but we, travelling people, treat them very seriously, believing that, on analysis, they reveal much of ourselves.

'So when I say "Pleasant dreams?" I really mean it.'

Lyonesse

It was the painter Charles Simpson who first really introduced me to the possibility of Lyonesse. He found the seas, that swarm around our Cornish coasts, a constant source of inspiration.

'The area of Cornwall which impresses the mind most strongly,' he reflected, 'with this peculiar quality of brooding, of vengeful menace . . . lies between the cliffs at Land's End and the narrow watershed some few miles nearer sunrise. Here the waves along two opposing coastlines strive which shall be first to wear down the resistance of the rocks and make an island of these westward hills . . . Fantasies of the past surge round its people as the great waters of the Atlantic surge round the soil they call their own.'

Lyonesse — they say — comprised of beautiful cities, rich and fertile plains: a land peopled by a noble race, whom one hundred and forty church towers summoned to worship.

Standing at the cliffs at Land's End, Lyonesse — for me — becomes a distinct possibility rather than just a story from legend. The tantalizing fascination about this lost land of Lyonesse is the enigma of it all: impossible and yet . . . Did Lyonesse once link Cornwall and the Scillies? Some people have said the Scillies *are* the high peaks of Lyonesse, and, of course, the rock formation around Land's End and that on Scilly *are* uncannily alike.

Legend handed down the generations gives us a pretty clear picture of the disaster: Trevilian — or Trevelyan — fleeing from Lyonesse on his white horse, the animal carrying its rider from a terrifying wall of water, the only survivors. The end of Lyonesse though was no sudden, dramatic deluge, for the explanation behind the successful escape of one man and his horse is that the man had shrewdly observed the sea making steady but dangerous inroads. Wisely, he moved his wife and family and livestock inland — to Cornwall — and when eventually disaster struck, in the form of a flood burst, the white horse galloped to safety, bringing his rider ashore at Perran. The interesting link with reality is that the Vyvyans, one of the most famous of Cornish families and landowners in Penwith for centuries, still have as their family crest a white horse saddled but minus rider: an artistic reminder of that famous white horse from Lyonesse. It's also said the Vyvyans kept a white horse in their stables at Trelowarren, on the mainland, saddled and waiting for any other such crisis. It may, of course, be only a good Cornish story, but either way, the white horse was never needed again.

Despite this long tradition of the lost land, history records no such disaster. But superstition is strong in Cornwall, and legends, like old soldiers, have a habit of refusing to die. Some have said that vegetation washed ashore in Mount's Bay was evidence of Lyonesse. One photograph, about 80 years old, portrays tree stumps uncovered in the bay. While the Victorian writer Robert Hunt wrote: 'I have passed in a boat from St Michael's Mount to Penzance on a summer's day, when the waters were very clear and the tide low, and seen the black masses of trees in the white sands extending far out into the bay.' Others remember Heath's words: '. . . at Sennen Church Town, near the extremity of Cornwall, there is a base of an old stone column belonging to a building which was taken up by some fishermen at the Place of the Seven Stones, about eighteen inches high and three feet in diameter at the circular base. Besides which, other pieces of buildings and glass windows have been taken up at different times in the same place with divers kind of utensils.'

The site of a once famous city is said to be marked by the Seven Stones reef, where in 1967 the gigantic oil tanker *Torrey Canyon* was wrecked with such disastrous results. Fishermen, from earlier times, said hereabouts they saw 'the roofs of churches, houses etc,' under the water on crystal-clear days. Some even maintained they had heard ghostly bells tolling. The distinguished Arthurian scholar Geoffrey Ashe has written '. . . much of this fantasy can be dismissed. The question is whether it all can . . .'

Geoffrey Ashe is wise to pose such a question, for Medieval

'When eventually disaster struck . . . the white horse galloped to safety . . .'▶

28

writers treated Lyonesse as an accepted geographical fact. Back in 1584 Norden, the celebrated map-maker, referred to Lyonesse in his *Description of Cornwall*, and that great chronicler Richard Carew in his *Survey of Cornwall*, wrote, 'The encroaching sea hath ravined from it the whole country of Lyonesse, together with divers other parcels of no little circuit, and that such a Lyonesse there was, these proofs are yet remaining . . .'

Sally Jones, in her *Legends of Cornwall*, which takes the shape of a journey through the legendary sites of this most westerly land, perceptively recalls Borlase's account of an earthquake in 1755 which killed three hundred thousand people in Portugal, and 'caused the seas off the west coast of Cornwall to rise by ten feet, and many people suggest that a similar phenomenon could have caused the seas to flood Lyonesse.

'On the Isles of Scilly themselves, crumbling stone walls and the foundations of buildings running mysteriously into the sea are still visible at low tide. Some Scillonians refer to the treacherous Seven

Below: 'Some have said that vegetation washed ashore in Mount's Bay was evidence of Lyonesse.' Right: 'Looking out from Land's End, I like to think Lyonesse belongs to reality.'

Stones Reef as "The Town", perhaps because the town of Lions is thought to have stood near the reef. This is just one of many mysteries.'

All of which brings us back to that vital question of how much can be dismissed as fantasy. Personally I seriously doubt whether all can be swept away. In researching Lyonesse I came across some extremely interesting observations by O.C.S. Crawford, the Editor of a *Quarterly Review of Archaeology,* housed in the Cornwall Library at Redruth. He attributed the Lyonesse story to 'the acute observations of fishermen and other unlettered folk. It is a common mistake to suppose that an "uneducated" person is less intelligent or less accurate in observation than one who has acquired book-knowledge. It would probably be more true to say that he is more intelligent and a better observer because his mind is clearer . . .

'In this instance, it seems to me probable that the legend arose somewhat after this fashion. Fishermen and others observed these walls . . . they recognised that they are of human making and they could not have been made when the land stood at its present level. They infer, quite correctly, that the land must have sunk. So far the inference is correct, and the process of reasoning could not be improved upon by the most eminent "highbrow".'

Lyonesse has triggered a good deal of thinking and writing over the years. A recent feature in *Cornish Life* by Donald Bray posed the question 'Where then lay the lost Land — if Lost Land there was? Westward or south'ard? Both or neither? There is so much to resolve, and the savants will be working on it, carbon dating and all. Recollections of a Britain land-linked to Europe, as it certainly was once, may indeed be fossilized in folk memory: Man has inhabited Earth a mighty long time. Trevelyan and Vyvyan traditions, legend, monkish gossip of long ago hint that Lyonesse stretched away into the sunset, and that Cornishmen, or their ancestors, tilled and built, hunted, loved, worshipped and fought there. What further proof should we incorrigible romantics ask?'

For some people, of course, Lyonesse simply exists in the realm of speculation. They may be right, but I believe Lyonesse, like Arthur himself, is in the field of probability.

◀ 'Those Medieval writers would surely have thought hard before making Lyonesse a geographical fact.'

I have to admit that, looking out from Land's End, I like to think Lyonesse belongs to reality; and that just isn't a Celt wanting things to fit neatly into the magical and mystical. In the course of writing two books on the Supernatural, and interviewing more than a hundred people on factual events that defy human explanation, I am less inclined to draw a line across words like possibility and probability — and Lyonesse is one case where I should seriously hesitate about precluding possibility.

Those Medieval writers would surely have thought hard before making Lyonesse a geographical fact.

Either way — fact or fiction — Lyonesse has now been woven into the fabric of Cornwall. The enigma of Lyonesse, the possibility and the improbability of it all, has a powerful fascination. Some cynics say Cornwall's wealth in legends is merely compensation for material poverty — an imaginary past making up for a real dearth.

Sit in a Cornish pub and the odds are you'll discover we're a country of story-tellers. Sit at the Minack Theatre, when a local company is performing or in one of our many town or village halls, and the chances are you'll see natural actors and actresses. The fate of all stories, and particularly legends, is that as they travel down the generations, they pick up different thoughts, different interpretations, succeeding writers or researchers adding a new moral perhaps, a new meaning.

So legends are an important part of our Cornish heritage, fanning the imagination of creative spirits, continuing to live on in the shape of music, poetry and prose.

Interestingly, Tennyson put Lyonesse in King Arthur territory:

So all day the noise of battle roll'd
Among the mountains by the winter sea;
Until King Arthur's table, man by man
Had fallen in Lyonesse, about their Lord
King Arthur . . .

Lyonesse, they say, died on a winter's night, and perhaps winter is the right season in which to seek the spirit of this lost land. 'Gone but not forgotten' is the sentiment expressed on many Cornish headstones — and that's precisely the case of Lyonesse. That noble land may have disappeared beneath the waves but it still excites curiosity and, strangely, is still very much alive.

Mysteries
in the Cornish Landscape

The Cornish landscape is not only mysterious in many places — parts of it remain a positive mystery. Take, for instance, those circles of standing stones, their true purpose will never be known. We suppose they were the meeting-places of an ancient people, but we only suppose. Religious or ceremonial perhaps? But again we only guess.

Anyway I decided to do a tour of just some of the mysteries in the Cornish landscape, and where better to begin than in the Hundred of Penwith, the most westerly corner of Cornwall? Filled with history and legend, Penwith — provided you have the humility to be still and listen — enables you to pick up echoes of long ago.

One of the most famous circles of all is the Merry Maidens in the Parish of St Buryan. You will find them beyond Lamorna, at Rosemodress; according to reliable archaeological opinion they form an almost perfect circle, so accurately are they placed.

Rex, my Welsh Collie Cross, and I have wandered around them on a cold still February morning and I was suddenly reminded of walking through Dame Barbara Hepworth's tropical gardens in St Ives: her sculptures — or some of them to me — gave the same impression of growing out of the Cornish landscape. 'The Cornish', she said, 'are an altogether sophisticated race; they've travelled as sailors, they've worked abroad as miners . . . they're very attuned to the universe.' Dame Barbara saw close parallels between this peninsula and her native West Riding. 'The landscape in both places possesses a tremendous power. Both places show the same type of scars in industrial developments. The people too have a good deal in common. They have an innate sense of craft. They know how to put a stone in a wall instinctively; it fits just right — and at the first attempt.'

Somebody has said that in Penwith you find yourself walking

among 'the early instalments of history,' and I knew exactly what he meant on that February morning. In a strange way though time seems to contract, and as when I meet Barbara Hepworth sculpture there is the temptation to handle and, in that moment of physical contact, a notion that in some curious way you are in touch with a distant power.

Betty Hill, formerly Paynter, had a vivid childhood memory concerning these Merry Maidens. 'It was the first war, and the landlord ordered the field to be ploughed, and they started trying to uproot one of the stones when the lead horse suddenly dropped dead. The whole thing was called off, and everybody started crossing themselves.'

Now the cynic may scoff. Personally I don't, for this landscape has a Supernatural quality.

These lovely weather-beaten stones inevitably feature in the legends of Cornwall. They are nineteen in all, and the legendary explanation is that these foolish maidens danced on a Sunday and, as a punishment, were transformed from human form to the stones that we see today. Not far away are the Pipers, two pillar stones, twelve feet high — these, they say, were the men who made the music for the dancing maidens — and suffered the same fate.

One of the most beautiful healing sites in all Cornwall, in my opinion, is also in Penwith. It's the Men-an-Tol standing on the moorland high above Madron. Men-an-Tol, in Cornish, means 'holed stone', and it's precisely that. This weather-beaten disc-shaped stone — again reminding me how Barbara Hepworth was often inspired to put the spirit and shape of Cornwall into her work — is pierced by a hole, big enough for most people to crawl through. And hundreds must have crawled through it over the years — not just for fun either — for the belief was that if you went through on all fours, you would be cured of many ills, and 'rickets' in particular. It stands flanked by two stones on one of the most awesome landscapes in the Hundred of Penwith. Away in the distance looms Ding Dong Mine: a reminder of Cornwall's mining past. Today Geevor is the only working mine in Penwith. I have stood here under a stormy January sky — grey clouds sweeping across the blue

'. . . those circles of standing stones, their true purpose will never be known.' ▶

and suddenly robbing the place of sunlight. Why here? And what is the purpose?

Peter Pool, the Penzance historian, believes the Men-an-Tol may have been a portal or entrance to the grave-passage of a barrow, the rest of which has now vanished.'

It's an intriguing thought.

Some maintain this stone has always stood in the ground as we see it today. Others disagree. Yet another group believes the Men-an-Tol must have some link with magic.

Certainly standing face to face with the Men-an-Tol, you realise the wisdom of Dr Johnson, when, long, long ago, he wrote: 'All that is really known of the ancient state of Britain is contained *in a few pages.'*

Dame Daphne du Maurier who loves Cornwall and knows the Celtic personality so well, in her brilliant *Vanishing Cornwall*, wrote of such landmarks and the response of the natives to them. 'Instinct, infallible, bade them place a hand upon the mound or stone, and spit. If the stone had a hole in it, like the Men-an-Tol, the wisest thing to do was to crawl through it nine times against the

Men-an-Tol: '. . . another group believes the Men-an-Tol must have some link with magic.'

sun. To crawl against the sun "blackened" the disease. The isolation
that kept Cornwall from the rest of England thus preserved an
ancient lore, an intuitive perception of things past . . . Those who
desire to understand the Cornish, and their country, must use their
imagination and travel back in time.'

Interestingly, belief in healing is very much alive. I know of
healers operating in the Westcountry, and all are regularly busy. So
perhaps something of that old faith — call it what you will —
remains in the bone.

From Penwith I moved up the county to Bodmin Moor. As the
Merry Maidens had drawn me down to West Cornwall, now another
kind of mini Stonehenge brought me back to the Moor.

This other famous ring is the Hurlers, near the village of Minions,
high on Bodmin Moor, or more precisely three adjacent rings. Again
apart from their sheer beauty, there is the alluring quality of the
unknown.

Sally Jones, in her *Legends of Cornwall*, has written of the
Hurlers' 'intangible power . . . Part of that power lies in their
mixture of mystery and significance, for although the stones are

**The Hurlers: '. . . apart from their sheer beauty, there is the
alluring quality of the unknown.'**

Hurling at St Columb: 'Once it was a popular sport but the Puritans condemned it.'

placed with scientific precision, their centres lying along a straight line, no one is entirely sure why they were erected or what strange ceremonies were enacted there long before the birth of Christianity.'

Once more legend insists that the stones were human beings turned to stone: punished for the act of rashly Hurling on the Sabbath. Hardly surprising then that Sunday sport came to Cornwall slowly, almost reluctantly.

Hurling's origin, like these stones, lies deep in Cornwall's past — not as deep but in some ways almost as vague and hazy, for some believe Hurling stems from the Bronze Age. Once it was a very popular sport but the Puritans condemned it.

In 1823 a boy, William Webb Ellis by name, picked up the ball, broke the law and ran with it across the turf of Rugby School, thereby creating the game of Rugby football. But here in Cornwall we like to think our Hurlers were the real pioneers of the great game, and we have some justification for an account of the sport by

Richard Carew, as long ago as 1602, uncannily anticipated some of Rugby's laws and patterns by more than two centuries.

Watching a horde of hurlers, charging up and down the streets of St Columb, chasing the elusive silver ball on Shrove Tuesday, I saw the natural relationship: Hurling, the primitive ancestor, and Rugby, the sophisticated offspring.

In the days of the first Elizabeth a Hurling match sometimes lasted two or three days. One chronicler recalled men 'returning home as from pitched batialle, with bloody pates, bones broken and out of joint, and such bruises as serve to shorten their days.'

C.E. Vulliamy though rated it highly: 'Across the slopes of the Moors, and through the fields beneath them, the men of Cornwall used to play their game of Hurling; the manliest, most glorious and exciting game that was ever played in Britain. It was an Homeric game, a game fit for heroes . . .'

I have stood on Bodmin Moor, by the Hurlers, and in the eye of my imagination, I have tried to see them.

These beautiful, ever-changing Moors must be haunted by many ghosts: the miners, the hurlers, the farmers, they all must people this landscape.

King Arthur's Downs: 'I found myself on the Arthurian trail again.'

Looking back, I realise I owe a lot to the painter and author Charles Simpson. Apart from stirring my interest in the possibility of Lyonesse, it was Charles Simpson who first opened my eyes to the magic of the Cornish Moors.

'Those who wander on the moors,' he told me, 'enter a domain of fog, shut out from the world of day among the shades of some dawn that never breaks, some paler counterpart of night. Sunsets there are, and golden skies, but they seem to be ruled by a capricious power who wills the sun to shine half in eclipse. The land has a countenance whose smiles only intensify its gloom and if there is laughter on the hills it's hollow as the cackle of an aged man.'

It was Charles Simpson too who taught me about the particular power of the Moor in the hour between sunset and darkness 'when ponies wander freely, foxes bark, animals call and only man wants to hide.'

Away on the other side of the Moor, I found myself on the Arthurian trail again. On Downs, that bear the great King's name,

Arthur at Court from a painting by Hatherell.

King Arthur's so-called Hall: '. . . nobody knows when these banks were built — or why?'

you will find King Arthur's Hall, another true Cornish mystery. The ruins of this manmade site, in the highest parish in Cornwall, St Breward, are often shrouded in a mist that clings to the roof of Cornwall — and the origin of the building is equally shrouded.

Arthur, of course, has become an international Agatha Christie theme — a detective operation, with scholars and archaeologists turning into Sherlock Holmes and Dr Watsons in an attempt to identify him — and to place him. But for all their efforts he remains an elusive, shadowy figure.

Personally I believe there was *an* Arthur — maybe not that Courtly figure in shimmering armour on a splendid charger, the picture in so many imaginations — but more a guerilla warfare fighter, rather like Tito in the last war. There are good historical grounds for placing Arthur here in the Westcountry, and Cornwall is fairly peppered with Arthurian place names. So again one wonders if there can be any smoke without fire.

Cornwall has her share of unanswered — in some cases unanswerable — questions, and King Arthur's so-called Hall here on the Moor is such a question. The plain fact is nobody knows when these banks were built — or why. They stand alone, rectangular on the skyline, approximately fifty yards along and twenty in width. Today, after centuries on this beautiful but bleak spot, they are weathered down to the height of a jockey, something like five feet. Today too the interior is fractionally lower than the surrounding moorscape, and it's partly under water.

Inside King Arthur's Hall, large stones were set up on end as a retaining wall, and something like three score are still in position. With the weathering of the bank beyond, they now stand freely, gaunt sculptures, on this lovely yet alien landscape, somehow generating the impression that you are standing inside some primitive temple — and maybe you are doing just that.

Not even the modern fencing around it can destroy this very primitive quality.

Brenda Duxbury and I on our Arthurian journey across Cornwall — *King Arthur Country in Cornwall* — pondered on the possibilities of this puzzling manmade site. 'Who were the people who went to this enormous effort? And why did they choose this exposed site on the top of Cornwall? Some say that it was a cattle pound, others a place of assembly, a cockfighting pit, or an earthwork occupied by a small detachment of Roman troops, but we think the most fitting explanation is a monument with ritualistic or burial undertones.'

In terms of sheer atmosphere, these Downs are older than Arthur's time. When I walked them, a while back, with Rex, as my only companion, they were cloaked in an aura of pre-history. As we moved across the coarse grass I *felt* I was walking back in time.

It must have been an assembly place of some kind, but the morning Rex and I were there, the only others present were Moorland cattle. There is a blackness about the Moor, and not just in the colour of the soil, many of the cattle who people it are black. The animals stared at us as if we were creatures from outer space.

In such a setting you realize how the Moor fans the imagination — and understand how it triggered such fine novels as *Jamaica Inn* by

King Arthur's Hall: 'Gaunt sculptures, on this lovely yet alien landscape.' ▶

Dame Daphne du Maurier and, more recently, *Chase the Wind* by E.V. Thompson. It is a wonder that the Moor has not been exploited more in paint. Turner, greatest of British painters, would surely have revelled in it on a stormy day, or with evening approaching and the sun flushing crimson away out over the Atlantic.

From King Arthur's Hall, I journeyed northward in the direction of Bossiney, the tiny hamlet that stands alongside Tintagel, facing the Atlantic Ocean.

Beyond Bossiney and below the coastal road leading to Boscastle is one of my favourite valleys. The Atlantic surges in and a river pours out, rendezvousing dramatically without a cove or spit of shore: Rocky Valley. The river, its identity totally and suddenly lost as it is swallowed by the ocean, had earlier plunged over St Nectan's forty foot waterfall into the kieve — the old Cornish word for basin. Canyon-like, vaguely Gothic, Rocky Valley is a setting possibly

Rocky Valley. Right: 'The Atlantic surges in and a river pours out.' Below: Carvings dating from the Bronze Age — 'Cornwall knows nothing like them.'

lifted from an Iris Murdoch novel. For me, an unexpected location and experience, somehow not quite Cornwall or Cornish.

Here in this dramatic valley is indeed a Cornish mystery or, more precisely, a brace of puzzles. Shaped into the Boscastle side of the valley, by the middle foot bridge, amidst ruins, are two rare Labyrinth Pattern Carvings, dating from the Early Bronze Age, approximately 1800 to 1400 years before the stable birth at Bethlehem.

Cornwall knows nothing like them, and their purpose remains shrouded in speculation. Whenever I venture down this lovely valley — and it's always a memorable experience — I look at this strange, ancient art work and wonder about the man or woman who carved it — and wonder whether these strange shapes are legacies of some distant magic or religion.

At Bossiney I heard an interesting account relating to the carvings. One curious searcher of the truth apparently persuaded a young woman to undergo hypnosis here on the spot — some form of regression, taking her back in time — and she emerged from the state of hypnosis in a very distressed condition, believing some form of human sacrifice had taken place. This may only have been village gossip as my informant was not able to give me either names or a date. Where I have been unable to obtain that kind of fact I have usually excluded, but, in this instance, my informant convinced me of his sincerity. He, at least, believed the horrifying hypnotic act occurred some years ago in the valley by these carvings.

A former neighbour of ours at Bossiney, Harvey Brown, a man who loved this area of North Cornwall, did show me notes made by the Cornish bard and author, the late W.H. Paynter, about the carvings. Bill Paynter wondered whether they marked a burial place in the valley. He mentioned that they resembled some found in Scotland — and those were said to represent a Mediterranean cult that had come to Scotland by the western approaches. As for their purpose, though, Bill Paynter had merely typed a significant question mark.

So they truly remain Cornish mysteries.

Now I moved down the coast to Portquin. At the edge of the

'Port Quin is a delightful mixture of beauty and mystery.' ▶

Atlantic, Portquin is a delightful mixture of beauty and mystery.

The tiny bay has a fiord-like face, a long finger of water cutting into this dramatic coastline. This, the third valley in St Endellion parish, running down to the Atlantic, was once a busy fishing village. But a story goes that, one night long, long ago, all the men of the village were drowned in a storm at sea — all perishing in the solitary boat owned by the village. The women and the children waited, but nobody returned from that ill-fated fishing trip — and Portquin became a ghost village, deserted by every inhabitant.

I say 'a story' because there are different theories about the death of Portquin. I have come here at evening, when the sun has slowly sunk beyond the rim of the Atlantic, and felt a strange melancholy hanging over the place. Standing on the cliffs as light ebbed from the sky, I remembered too a Canadian who firmly believed he was a son of Portquin, or, more accurately a descendant, his theory being that, back in the last century, the population of Portquin emigrated

Port Quin: '. . . a long finger of water cutting into this dramatic coastline.'

'This North Cornish coast and the Atlantic are littered with wrecks and ghosts.'

to Canada. A possibility of course.

Did a combination of a poor fishing season and failure of local mining combine to send the men of Portquin somewhere else? That's yet another possibility. Or did the men all get cornered by a Press Gang and meet some later even more cruel fate? Other people though look for a more materialistic reason: that fishing around the corner at Port Isaac looked a better proposition — and the villagers simply left.

That may be so, but nobody can doubt the strong possibility of a fishing boat being lost at sea; for this North Cornish coast and the Atlantic are littered with wrecks and ghosts. The bitter truth is the North coast of Cornwall is fiendishly inhospitable to ships and sailors in trouble. Vessels caught in foul weather have often tried to find refuge in the Camel Estuary only to be driven on to the notorious Doom Bar. Doom is an apt name for more boats have been wrecked thereabouts than any other comparable area in Cornwall. Clive Carter, in his book *Cornish Shipwrecks*, puts the figure at three hundred boats in one hundred and fifty years. Against a backcloth of figures like those, no Cornishman would completely discount the strong possibility of the tragedy of Portquin.

The National Trust has helped to resurrect the village by converting the old fishermen's cottages into holiday accommodation. While on Doyden Point, there is a vivid reminder of Cornwall's ability to astonish: a beautiful Regency Gothic folly — that was used in the brilliant Poldark series on BBC television. A more improbable site for such architecture is difficult to imagine.

But for me the magic of this place is its sheer beauty and the horrific yet distinct possibility of that tragic first story. You feel it could have happened here, and perhaps Sir John Betjeman pinned the mood to paper when he wrote 'High hills enclose the sea which seems to be licking its chops and thirsting for more lives.'

Charming and Premonitions

Rightly or wrongly, I have always looked upon charming as a kind of magic. Maybe that's the Celt and the Cornishman finding a fascination in things the scientist cannot explain.

Charming may not be as old as Rough Tor or Brown Willy, but the practice goes back many, many generations. Scholars and surgeons in the 1300s referred to the employment of charms; so folk medicine has undoubtedly played a significant background role in the unfolding of medical history.

Not many years ago Cornwall was well populated with charmers — 'white witches' they were called — but nowadays they've become a rare breed. And my appointment to meet one took me once more across the beautiful, brooding moors of Bodmin to Common Moor, a hamlet below the Hurlers and Minions. The cottages and houses nestle in a sheltered valley, and the 'No through Road' sign probably helps to give it a privacy that many other Cornish villages would envy.

Violet Joan Bettinson lives at Rosevale, an old miner's cottage — back in the early 1800s this was booming mining country — nearby a tiny stream journeys its way to meet the beautiful River Fowey at Draynes. Joan Bettinson has those blue eyes that I now immediately, instinctively look for in psychic people. Certainly within a matter of minutes of meeting her, you realise you're in the presence of an extraordinary person. She speaks slowly, the pitch is low; she weighs words carefully: no hint of exaggeration.

With her Siamese cat curled contentedly on my lap, and her dog stretched out before the fire, I asked her how she began charming.

'It's strange really . . . as a young girl I had warts on my hand, as many young girls do. Now though my grandmother charmed warts, I decided to charm them away myself. So I got a piece of raw meat

and rubbed it over the warts and then threw the piece of meat over my left shoulder. It's a fact the warts shrivelled and eventually disappeared.'

Oddly, though, Joan Bettinson then seemingly forgot all about charming. It had worked for her as a young girl — and that was that. 'It wasn't until 1955 that I started charming properly, and it all came about quite by accident. I was the last lady postman to do the Fowey Valley on foot and by bike . . . I rate the Fowey Valley a magical place. Well, this farmer was really worried about his cattle. The herd had got a lot of ringworm. "Us have tried everything, maid. Do you know anybody who can charm them?" he said. There and then I decided "I'll try!" I looked at the cattle in the field; they were in two or three groups, and I willed them to be better. "They'll go in ten days," I told him, "but when they do, don't thank me." And sure enough, one day he stopped me with the news! "They be gone, maid. Not a bit of ringworm on any of them." And he was wise enough not to thank me either. He assured me too that he hadn't used any further treatment. He'd just relied on my charming, and it had worked.'

And from then she's gone on charming ringworm from cattle and warts from human beings. She doesn't advertise the fact. News of her powers travels by that very efficient network in Cornwall we call 'bush telegraph'.

'I think one of the worst cases I met was a retired market gardener from Calstock. He had warts so bad on both hands that you couldn't get a pin between them. "I'm ashamed to show my hands in public," he confessed. "I've tried everything under the sun, but they're just as bad." Well, I said I'd try . . . and about a fortnight later I met him and he showed me his hands. They were better, better than they'd been. . . but quite a few warts remained. . . and for the only time in my life I charmed the same warts a second time. It was about six weeks later that I saw him coming down the road. When he saw me, he held out both hands. There was not a single wart on either hand!'

Perhaps even more incredibly Joan Bettinson has cured shingles. 'I've done it for a relative in Torquay, and others, without even going to see them . . . yes, a kind of absent healing . . . I did it too for

◄ **Cornish charmer, Joan Bettinson, lives at Rosevale.**

someone as far away as London. I picture the person and picture them rid of the warts or shingles. Distance doesn't matter . . . you have to *see* the person and the trouble gone.'

She doesn't pray or use any kind of ritual. 'I'm not over-religious she admits, 'though I've been happy worshipping with Methodists and Church of England.'

On her post-delivery journey, one day in 1957, Joan Bettinson had a vivid premonition that a certain young person would not live beyond a certain age. 'A fleeting thought or voice had whispered and yet imprinted on my mind that I shall never forget it . . . and nearly twenty years on I heard of the passing of that particular person and when I read the obituary in the local paper, the age was absolutely right!'

I could show you the very spot where I was standing in the Valley when the thought suddenly struck . . .

Joan Bettinson loves this Fowey Valley, and it surely is one of the most beautiful in all Cornwall. 'Well, some years ago the Valley, or "up the bottoms", as it's known locally was under the threat of being flooded, so with all the psychic power at my command I willed that the flooding would not happen . . . and none took place.'

It was back in 1930 that her late father — she's a member of the old Cornish family of Marrack who hailed from Castallack, Paul, in West Cornwall — bought the Reverend Samuel Catts's Chapel, a Wesleyan Reform building, constructed here in the village in 1854, that had closed as a place of worship during the 1914-18 War.

'The story goes that Samuel Catts, the Wesleyan Minister, had gone astray and got a servant girl pregnant. That was a great disgrace in those days, and though he was dismissed from the Ministry he remained very popular with the miners on the Moor . . . and the place has always been known as Catts' Chapel.

'Many strange things happened during my time at the Chapel (it's now called Glensilva, the home of her sister Mary Marrack) and my late mother often wondered if it was because we were on consecrated ground. One evening during the winter of 1932, we were sitting in the dining room there, and we all heard a loud thump above. I took a candlestick and went upstairs, and there was a pink and white jug, not broken but on the floor, handle upward . . . an unseen hand had lifted it out of the basin and placed it on the floor. "Don't tell me," Father said, "I know what *that* means!"

'Soon after my father became bedridden and I often was sent up

56

Catts' Chapel: 'Many strange things happened . . .'

with a clome hot water bottle for his feet. On one occasion, I reached the landing when suddenly the door opened of its own accord without a draught . . . I dropped the bottle and ran down to my mother. Then, one morning, we came downstairs to find the lovely epergne (centre piece) on the dining room table in two parts, as if somebody had cut it in half! A few weeks later mother and I were cooking in the kitchen when we both heard a loud smashing of glass, as if a hundred lamp glasses had been smashed on a stone floor. We searched the house from top to bottom but there was no sign of glass anywhere . . . only a week later my father passed away.'

Some strange premonitions took place in the old chapel during the last war. One June morning a large mug was seemingly lifted by invisible hands and laid on its side and on another occasion a bird came up to the kitchen window, flapping its wings hard against the glass. Both events more or less coinciding with deaths in the family. If Joan Bettinson were not so psychic, one might have dismissed such happenings as pure coincidence. She, for her part, believes in omens. For example, back in the early 1930s her sister returned home one morning to fetch something she had forgotten — and that very day her sister sustained a terrible accident, losing nearly all her left hand.

More recently both sisters were associated with another strange omen. 'My sister Mary was filling her hot water bottle one dark November night, her television set was on upstairs, when all of a sudden she heard a loud thumping on the stairs . . . she ran out to see what it was and found a very heavy crucifix which stood well-back in the staircase window. It had somehow bounced down the stairs. (The window from which the crucifix had fallen was the original Chapel window.) Mary was so frightened that she came running over to me here at Rosevale. We could not think how this could have happened but when we heard next day about the assassination of President Kennedy of the United States, we worked out the time and it would have been exactly the time when he was shot. Of course we shall never know what connection that family had, but maybe back in the nineteenth century someone of that family may have been known or associated with one of the old miners who had emigrated to America during the Depression as did so many Irish people.'

Perhaps inevitably our conversation then turned to clairvoyancy. Though she practises the art of prophecy, Joan Bettinson normally only does it for charitable causes. However as a way of saying 'Thank you' for the gift of two books, she proceeded to make some forecasts for me and as with her charming, there was no ritual — either using tarot cards or gazing into a crystal. She merely studied her hand and without looking at me proceeded to make something like half a dozen predictions in her quiet deliberate way. Some seemed beyond the bounds of all possibility, but having worked with Acora I have learnt never to contradict or limit possibilities.

I drove back up the Fowey Valley, with the sun beginning to slip Westward, feeling that I had just met a woman with extraordinary power — and perception.

'I recognise signs as did the three wise men in Biblical times so I don't think it's wicked as some people suggest,' she had said. 'And I feel I get this psychic something from someone who has passed on.'

Joan Bettinson is probably right — and in that last sentence she reminded me that death itself remains perhaps the most tantalizing mystery of all. As a result of my researches into the Supernatural, I am quite convinced that death is not the end, but a door opening — admittedly leading to somewhere we know little about — and therein lies great mystery.

Did Christ Come to Cornwall?

When we think or talk of Jesus Christ, we come to the biggest mystery of all: God in human form, triumphing over the thing we call death and proving the reality of eternal Life. That has been the belief and conviction of millions of men and women, within the framework of the Christian Faith, for a span of all but two thousand years.

And interestingly within a Cornish context we come to an absolutely fascinating question: Did Christ, as a boy, come to Cornwall?

There is a legend, bordering on a mixture of hope and belief, that the young Jesus did precisely that. There are various versions but the basic story is Jesus came to Cornwall with Joseph of Arimathea on a tin-buying venture. It is believed Joseph was an uncle of Mary, the mother of Jesus. Joseph was more than a wealthy trader and merchant, he was a skilful sailor and navigator. So it was natural he should suggest the boy Jesus should come with him on one of his voyages. And, of course, it is historically feasible.

After all, Blake, the mystic, wrote those stirring words:

> *And did those Feet in ancient time*
> *Walk upon England's mountains green*
> *And was the Holy Lamb of God*
> *On England's pleasant pastures seen?*

In my days as a schoolmaster at St Erbyn's School, Penzance, then under the Headmastership of Rex Carr, every school term ended with that rousing, moving hymn. And, of course, Blake's imagination had been fired by this lovely tradition which every true Cornish man or woman hopes is genuine.

Jane Oliver, in a book entitled *In No Strange Land*, published in the 1940s, makes Joseph on a later visit say: 'He loved the country

PIRAN-BISHOP 15.10.80

and its little creatures. I always knew that he saw every stirring thing, though I, may I be forgiven, tried to turn his mind to the business through which I had made my wealth. But he only smiled at my talk of ingots and miners' wages. The fishermen now, he was far more interested in them.' That certainly is a picture that will appeal to all who cherish the Christ in Cornwall story.

But alas as with Arthur we lack any reliable written record. As with Arthur too the tradition is not restricted to just one part of Cornwall — indeed Somerset also claims it.

There are, of course, intriguing links. Arthur's quest for the Holy Grail is central to the whole Arthurian theme, and legend maintains that the Chalice, used by Christ at the Last Supper, was brought to this country by the same Joseph of Arimathea.

Times were when I saw fact and legend inside clearly defined areas, but the older I get the less certain I become about the clarity of some definitions. Indeed I seriously doubt whether there be any total myth, no shred of reality.

Wallace Nichols, the poet and novelist who lived and wrote in the

Left: 'Did Christ as a boy come to Cornwall?' Below: Place Manor 1914. 'There is a magical atmosphere about Place.'

Penzance area for many years, was another whose imagination was fanned by this Christ theme in Cornwall. He wrote a Dramatic Morality in Two Acts, entitled *The Boy from Egypt,* and said it was 'based on a persistent legend that runs in Cornwall'. Wallace Nichols, whom I got to know well in the last years of his life, was a stickler for accuracy. He therefore always stressed that it was 'symbolic drama with its roots in legend'.

David Mudd too, in his seventh Bossiney title, *Around & About The Roseland,* has mentioned that Christ's visit may be only a legend, 'but perhaps the Saints, the churches, and the quiet reverence that is so obvious throughout the Roseland even in these modern times stem from a chance visit two thousand years ago'.

I know exactly what David Mudd meant when he wrote about that 'quiet reverence' for, one Saturday morning in high summer, I came to Place Manor — now a hotel — and it was close on noon, the hotel bustling with staff and guests and children playing happily and noisily on the green lawns that go down to the water. Here at Place you gain access to the little Church of St Anthony by literally walking through the hotel kitchen. Naturally enough, the kitchen staff were busy, preparing for lunch, and yet within seconds I found myself inside the church and enveloped in a beautiful peace — only a few feet away from all the material matters of hotel business, food and drink — and yet in another Roseland world. After a few minutes in that quiet, darkened church I emerged feeling better, somehow more whole. There is a magical atmosphere about Place — little wonder it was frequently quoted as the site of Christ's landing in Cornwall.

I say 'was quoted' because there is a feeling that the Holy Legend is less talked about among Cornish folk these days. A decline in congregations? Or fear of ridicule from sophisticated sceptics? Maybe a little of both.

Place is not the only Roseland spot to make this particular claim. Beautiful St Just-in-Roseland is another. I have heard of a local preacher who talked with old inhabitants, convinced that Christ had been here — even to the extent of indicating a flat stone on which He had stepped when he came ashore.

If the boy Christ did pull into this beautiful Roseland creek, then St Just was probably the religious centre for the area. Anyway the fascinating theory is that Jesus talked with the Druids — in much the same style as he had conversed with the leaders of the Temple —

62

thus paving the path for the coming of Christianity.

Further up the coast is another possible Jesus site. At the eastern tip of the mouth of the River Fowey is a colony of rocks, and on the biggest rock is an improbable wooden cross. 'Punche's Cross', they call it, and that's been its name for a long time, way back in 1525 the historian Leland referred to it by that name. Why here? And what does it represent? Those are good questions, for it marks nothing sombre like a grave or a wreck. The story, handed down the ages, is that Jesus came ashore with his uncle to inspect the mines.

But — and it's an intriguing but — there is a second tradition surrounding this lonely wooden cross. The second theory is that at a later date Pontius Pilate landed here — 'Punche's' is said to be a form of corruption of the Roman word 'pontius'. Here theory is not stretching our imagination or reasoning too far because Pilate *was* a Foreign Service officer or diplomat. Furthermore after the sensational events relating to the Crucifixion Pilate became an

St Just-in-Roseland: '. . . the Saints, the churches and the quiet reverence . . .'

'. . . inevitably Looe Island features on the Cornish list.'

intensely unpopular figure in Judea — so unpopular that he was almost certainly transferred overseas — a political tactic, well-employed and known in our day. Some reports say he was sent to Switzerland and France. Again it is within the bounds of feasibility that Pilate could later have been sent to Britain — to Cornwall — which was the furthest Roman Province from Jerusalem — and, of course, furthest from all the controversy. So it is possible that these two great rival New Testament characters came ashore at — or near — 'Punche's Cross'.

Islands are among the most romantic characters on any map; so perhaps inevitably Looe Island features on the Cornish list. Standing roughly a mile from the fishing port of Looe, the island has distant views of the high ground above Liskeard: the old mining country of St Cleer which, of course, brings us back to Joseph of Arimathea and his mining connections. Other mining territory, where the Christ tradition has been mentioned, includes that around Redruth and St Day and rugged, ancient Ding Dong Mine down in Penwith.

Canon Jennings, in his *Madron, Morvah & Penzance,* has suggested that the tradition of Christ coming into Mount's Bay is the possible explanation for the name of the town of Penzance, meaning 'Holy Headland'. While yet another version is that Joseph brought both Mary and the boy Jesus ashore at St Michael's Mount. The Mount was naturally an important landmark and could logically have been the scene of such a landing two thousand years ago. According to the Greek chronicler, Diodorus Siculus, tin was collected at St Michael's Mount and then despatched to Morlaiz, from where it was taken by packhorse to Marseilles — and finally shipped to Phoenicia.

There is undoubtedly a spiritual, even Supernatural quality about the Mount. How the Mount got its name is another area of choice. One theory is that St Michael appeared in a vision to a hermit of the Mount: an event that inspired Milton to produce *The great vision of the guarded mount.* The second theory is that St Michael appeared in a vision to a group of local fishermen who saw him standing on a rock on this island in 495 — which brings us back to Arthur's times. On any exploration of Cornwall, it seems impossible to avoid that great character.

Did Christ — as a boy — sail up the Camel? That's another traditional question.

Above: The River Camel. Right: St Michael's Mount.

The River Camel begins its life high above the town of Camelford: a small streamlet trickles across soggy yet harsh landscape, the beginning of its journey to join the Atlantic beyond Doom Bar. Our faces are moulded by our past, and the same is true of places. Down the centuries, merchant and invader, missionary and immigrant have all sailed along the Camel. Apart from Hayle near St Ives, this is the only estuary to offer refuge in a storm on this notorious north coast of Cornwall.

The Camel Valley has always been an important route to the south coast, linking with the River Fowey. From Prehistoric times, travellers from Ireland and Wales used this way thereby avoiding the possibly dangerous rounding of Land's End, and once on the south coast, they could embark again for Brittany, the Continent and even the Mediterranean. And this was not a one-way flow, for the lure of tin and copper brought many across the Channel as well as the Irish Sea.

The North Cornwall version is that the boy Jesus came ashore at St Minver to get fresh water for the ship, and here you will find the only place on the map of Cornwall that bears his name. Standing in the middle of a field, Jesus Well still provides a water supply.

The Quiller Couches, on a visit in the 1890s, discovered that children suffering from whooping cough were still taken to drink the waters . . . 'pins were dropped in for the telling of fortunes and even money was cast into its depths for the same reason . . . one particular Sunday . . . as much as sixteen shillings were taken out by unbelievers who then reaped the benefit of the superstitions of others.'

These then are a whole range of Cornish locations, claiming an earthly link with Christ.

Finally, however, I found myself going back to St Just-in-Roseland. The fact is the sheer beauty of the place — it *is* a Garden of Eden — makes you believe *anything* could have happened here. Yet apart from the beauty and the power of the atmosphere, there are good reasons for supposing Christ could have come ashore here on the south coast — and one man who takes that line is the Reverend Peter Durnford, the Rector of St Just-in-Roseland since 1970 and a former Royal Naval officer.

Jesus Well: 'Jesus came ashore at St Minver . . .' ▶

'In addition to the places you've mentioned,' he told me, 'there have been claims for Falmouth and Mylor.' Peter Durnford thinks there could be a reasonable explanation for more than one landing site. 'You must remember ships, in those days, didn't have radar and all the sophisticated equipment and navigational aids of today. Equally important there were no charts of any great precision. You could have aimed for Falmouth and easily ended up at Looe and, of course, there could have been more than one visit as Joseph is thought to have regularly traded with Cornwall. So I don't necessarily see any contradiction because there's more than one site.'

He feels strongly though that St Michael's Mount is not a probable site. 'If you were coming to Britain, then only a clot would have headed for Mount's Bay. The ships would have been fairly big and there would have been the danger of being embayed, the prevailing wind being from the south west . . . something every sailor dreaded . . . and there's little shelter in Mount's Bay in bad weather. Speaking as a sailor, I'd plump for the Falmouth area. It makes better geographical and historical sense. Then the rivers went deeper inland and ships went as far up as Tregony. There are many pointers suggesting St Just-in-Roseland, this wonderfully sheltered creek; you could get water here and timber for any repairs. There's this ancient look-out we have, and a tin ingot was dredged up off St Mawes Point. So you have genuine historical elements. Then there are other pointers, admittedly emotional but no weaker for that. This isn't something dead that you can stick a pin into, and make a definite decision in an instant. Above all, you've got this legend that won't go away and the living tranquillity of St Just. It's all perfectly feasible . . . Christ could have come to Cornwall and I believe St Just is a better proposition than anywhere else in Cornwall.'

Finally, I asked about that flat stone where, some said, Christ had stepped ashore. 'Great secrecy has gone on amongst the locals about the legend and the stone in particular. I've never seen it, but they say the stone was here one day and gone the next . . . there's no explanation.'

Later I stood by the lychgate and looked down, once more, to the Church below and the creek beyond. This is surely one of the most magical places in all Cornwall and if Christ did come to Cornwall, then it deserves to have been here.

Controversy and Clerics

Cornwall has had more than her share of eccentrics. There was the Perpetual Curate of Gunwalloe, who seen genuflecting when passing the stalls' gangway of a London theatre was told 'You're not at Mass!' — and who sharply retorted 'Everything's Mass to me!'

More recently there has been the St Ives fisherman Alfred Wallis. Living like a hermit in a tiny cottage in Back Road West, and considered 'touched' by some of his neighbours, Wallis started painting at the age of seventy. Using ordinary household paints on bits of cardboard, he began producing childlike pictures which today are regarded as among the most brilliant primitive paintings. In his lifetime he gave many away, and sold others for only a few shillings. Like the Cornish carver of earlier times, Burnard of Altarnun, Wallis died penniless in a workhouse: two incredible yet tragic Westcountry tales.

Happily, too, eccentricity is not entirely something of the distant past. Sonia and I fondly recall our former Port Isaac fishman who firmly declined 'to go decimal'. He was convinced decimalization wouldn't 'catch on' and insisted on continuing to give us our prices in pounds, shillings and pence! We also knew a fiercely independent lady in Bossiney who proudly displayed a notice in her front window: 'This cottage is not for sale.' No exclamation mark, you'll note. And there was a corpulent Cornish farmer, who usually worked on the farm in his old Sunday best, but when it came to rain he'd shed his shirt, jacket, waistcoat and trousers — hiding them under the hedge or under a sack — and then proceed to go about his business in only vest and underpants, socks and boots. I never had the good fortune to see this particular performance — but was assured it was standard practice.

Of all the clerics, who people Cornish history, two are famous for

Robert Stephen Hawker — 'a legend in his lifetime.'

the eccentric way they lived — and, to a degree, the strange way they died: both controversial and both Anglicans.

First, let us go to Morwenstow, that wild, windswept parish in North Cornwall where Robert Stephen Hawker became a legend in his lifetime. Here Hawker lived, preached, wrote and worked for forty-one years. Parson and poet, creator of the modern Harvest Festival Service and designer of the Gothic-like Morwenstow Vicarage, he was a man of numerous parts. This wicked North Cornish coast has finished many fine ships, and Hawker's exploits coping with shipwrecks alone assured him of a substantial place in Cornish history.

On one occasion, he wrote of being roused at first light of day by a boy: 'In a moment, I was up, and in my cassock and slippers rushed out. There stood my lad, weeping bitterly, and holding out to me in his trembling hands a tortoise, alive. I found afterwards that he had grasped it on the beach, and brought it in his hands as a strange and marvellous arrival from the waves, but in utter ignorance of what it might be.

'I ran across my glebe, a quarter of a mile, to the cliffs, and down a frightful descent of three hundred feet to the beach. It was, indeed, a scene to be looked at only once in human life. On a ridge of rock, just left bare by the falling tide, stood a man, my own servant: he had come out to see my flock of ewes, and found this awful wreck. There he stood, with two dead sailors at his feet, whom he had just drawn out of the water, stiff and stark.'

There was though another side to the wrecks, for it's been said that Mr Hawker was not averse to 'salvaging' the occasional cask of brandy.

Of his Churchmanship to say that he was High is to oversimplify. He revered the Blessed Virgin, the ideal of womanhood appealed to the poet inside the priest, and his devotion to the Church of England was mainly based on a conviction that St Morwenna came from Ireland and that the Irish received their Christian Faith from the early Eastern Church, and not the Church of Rome. But he was complex. There was, for example, something of the Calvanist in his make-up, and on some religious matters he could be intolerant. He had little time for the Methodists, and once when questioned about the qualities of John Wesley, he replied: 'Tell me about Wesley when you can give me his present address.'

Certain parts of Cornwall have a haunted, haunting quality and this is especially true of Morwenstow. Therefore I was not surprised to encounter genuine claims of ghostly experiences in this area.

Mrs Constance Drummond of Stratton told me of an occurrence between the two wars. 'One evening a friend and I were walking back from Morwenstow with my retriever dog. We *both* heard footsteps behind us. There was a corner, and we both paused. I said: "Oh, let's wait for whoever it is to pass." We stopped, and noticed that my dog had flattened himself into the hedge. The footsteps came on round the corner, passed us, and went on. No one to be seen. At a cottage higher up, I asked a woman if the lane was haunted. "Oh, yes," she said brightly, "Parson Hawker often comes up after being at the church . . ."'

I then asked Joan Rendell, the author of *Hawker Country,* about the possibility of Hawker haunting his old parish. Joan Rendell, apart from being very psychic, and a font of wisdom on the great man, knows this territory well and feels an attunement with

Morwenstow Church: '. . . parts of Cornwall have a haunted, haunting quality . . .'

Hawker. As she once put it: 'All of us have our little personal foibles and fancies, what in Cornwall we call "quaims"; all of us have something of the eccentric in us, whether we like to admit it or not; let us say that Mr Hawker could be reincarnated in many of us.'

Anyway she was under no illusions about the ghostly claims. 'While I was doing the research for my book *Hawker Country* several people assured me perfectly seriously that they believed Mr Hawker haunted the parish of Morwenstow. One elderly lady who lived for many years in Morwenstow but has now left the parish told me that she had always felt Hawker's presence in church during services and she said that she always felt an urge to glance in the direction of the spot in the church where Hawker had expressed a wish to be buried. This lady said that she felt Hawker was beckoning to her to look in that direction. "I quite missed him when I left Morwenstow," she said seriously. Another lady said quite casually that she had "often seen Mr Hawker" walking along one of the lanes which he frequented in life. She said there was nothing scary about it, in fact, she seemed to regard it as a pleasant meeting with an old friend and I had the impression that she felt quite disappointed if she walked that lane and didn't see Mr Hawker. Several times I encountered this everyday attitude to what can only be described as a ghost but which no one referred to as such. They all spoke as though Mr Hawker was still a living person. If he really does come back to visit his old favourite spots he must be delighted to know that he is received so favourably!'

Hawker's life, in places, reads like fiction rather than genuine biography. Typical was his first marriage. When he was nineteen, his aunt sent him to Oxford, but she soon died and his father an impoverished curate, could not afford the fees. His University career looked doomed. Hawker however found the fees and a solution in marriage. He promptly went off to Bude and proposed to his godmother, a lady of forty-one, who accepted.'

The influence of Charlotte Hawker on his life was considerable. A woman of poetic, refined mind, she helped him through periods of depression and gave him sound guidance when impetuosity threatened his judgment. She died at the age of eighty-one; her grave is at Morwenstow, outside the chancel. Charlotte's passing wounded him deeply; depression closed in, he moped about, seemingly interested in little. Sciatica plagued him, and he turned to opium. But in the following year he found himself a second wife, a

Pole who bore him three daughters.

His last years, though, were unhappy. His health declined seriously, the prospects of his family oppressed him, anxieties gnawed. In June, 1875, he stayed with his brother at Boscastle, who, in a letter, described him as 'very ill, and certainly broken in his mind'. By the end of August, Robert Stephen Hawker was in his coffin in Plymouth Cemetery — a Roman Catholic. His end is cloaked in confusion and controversy.

The second Mrs Hawker — Pauline — had taken him to Plymouth for medical advice. There he had suffered a paralytic stroke, and on the Saturday before his death, Mrs Hawker sent for the Roman Catholic, Canon Mansfield. She later insisted that such an invitation was at the request of her husband. Sabine Baring-Gould, though, in his biography *The Vicar of Morwenstow* clearly stated: 'Through the kindness of Mr Hawker's relatives I have been furnished with every letter that passed on the subject of his death, and reception into Roman communion. In not one of them is it asserted that he asked to have Canon Mansfield sent for: the last expression of a wish was that he might go back to Morwenstow.'

Baring-Gould's biography, it is fair to say, does contain some inaccuracies. But that wish to 'go back to Morwenstow' has an authentic ring. Hawker, after all, had given forty-one years of his life to the parish. Nevertheless Pauline Hawker should have known her husband's innermost thoughts. Or did she? Her belief was that he had been 'at heart a Roman Catholic' for some years.

Was Hawker capable of making a decision to join the Roman Catholic Church at this sick, late stage in his life? Or did he hang on at Morwenstow because he loved the place so? Or did he stay for purely material reasons? Or did he profess Roman Catholicism privately and yet publicly perform as an Anglican parson?

These are only some of the questions that shape themselves in what was a religious row and remains a riddle surrounding Hawker's earthly end. We shall probably never now get to the bottom of it. This much though is certain: in the hearts of many Cornish people, Hawker will — for ever — be the Vicar of Morwenstow.

◄Joan Rendell: '. . . several people assured me they believed Mr Hawker haunted the parish of Morwenstow.'

Eccentricity and the Cornish clergy have frequently gone together, almost as naturally as strawberries and Cornish cream.

One wealthy Cornish parson, asked by his butler 'What wine for Communion tomorrow, sir?' replied 'Oh, give 'em hock for a change!'

To follow in the footsteps of our second controversial clergyman though, we veer back inland. Warleggan stands on the south-eastern fringe of Bodmin Moor, roughly a mile — as the Cornish Chough presumably flew — from Dozmary Pool, that lovely sheet of water where some say Sir Bedivere grudgingly threw away the magical sword Excalibur.

Even today Warleggan has an isolated air, an impression intensified by the remote farms of slate and granite, and high-hedged lanes that shut out the view until they climb to the Moor and disappear. It must have appeared even more isolated to Frederick William Densham when he arrived in 1931. And before he died in 1953, Densham had become as isolated as the landscape.

It is a curious story — a sad one too — and could perhaps have only happened here in Cornwall. Who better to tell the greater part of this strange tale than Laura Farnworth who lived here at Warleggan Rectory and made a special study of the Rectory's most famous, or infamous resident.

Within the old Rectory big red crosses are painted upon most of the upstairs doors. Upon each cross is written, in capitals, a Biblical name, such as Pizgah, Emmaus and Cyprus. Bolts are fixed upon the outsides of the doors while some windows bear as many as five catches. The crosses and their names are cracked and darkened, but vivid still; and the rows of catches are there also.

Densham, himself, created the strange scene.

At the time of his appointment, the patron of the living was not known locally, and so the new incumbent was an utter stranger, unknown to the Parish Church Council. Very necessary was it for him to win, if not the hearts, at least the acceptance of his flock; and while he was doing so his past would offer, no doubt, fertile soil for speculation and rumour. Such interest is understandable enough in so remote a parish as Warleggan. Here, if you glance at the Church register or at the headstones in the graveyard, you see the same names recurring again and again out of the years and you realize the rarity of a stranger, what a delight to local tongues he would be.

The verdict on Densham was that obviously he had never worked in a rural parish before. Several incautious actions showed this. For example, he very soon bought a litter of puppies, with no thought evidently, agreed his parishioners, of the havoc a pack of dogs can cause in a farming community, particularly one where the economy centred on sheep.

If you explore Warleggan Rectory, wander through its thirteen rooms, up and downstairs, you realise its size. The grounds too are extensive. Great rhododendrons, tossing pink and purple in the summer, flank the drive, while around are tall beeches, gay also on a bright day when their colony of rooks is busy and talkative about domestic affairs. But in winter the scene is different indeed. Then those beeches look rather like a huge elbow crooked protectively around the Rectory and sheltering it from the wind, rushing cold and rain-laden from the moors; the midday sky may be dark . . . a darkness that seems to move nearer as you watch it . . . and at such a time you can only wonder how a man, knowing nobody in the parish, would feel alone in the many rooms of that house. Not one neighbourly light, even, was visible from its windows. Densham's purchase of the dogs is understandable. It illustrates also that impulsiveness which alienated people from the start.

As a clergyman he would already have moved several times in his life and taken leadership of people he scarcely knew. A parish of Cornish farmers, however, needed a specially cautious approach. Such dour men, caring nothing about their impression on Densham, took for granted that *they* did the accepting. But he was not tentative at all towards them. At his first Parochial Church Council meeting he made several proposals 'carried *nem. con.*, there being no response'. So from the beginning Warleggan was granite towards him. They resented his overriding of their opinions and some Council members ceased to attend meetings. For this, Densham removed their names from the Parish Church electoral roll.

However, the bond between priest and flock remained in place — until two crucial events took place.

First the pups had grown. They were the Rector's companions in the lonely house, and he had affectionately honoured the largest by bestowing on him the name of Gandhi, his hero. What a shock when one day news came that his dogs were running across the moor slaughtering sheep, peaceful Gandhi their leader.

Whatever happened on that occasion, the dogs did cause damage at times and Mr Densham paid heavily, in money and congregation. Several farmers ceased to attend services — and several farmers meant quite a falling off in so small a community. Others demanded that the dogs be put down. Densham's servants now urged that the Rectory grounds, all three and a half acres, should be totally fenced, to keep in the dogs. The Rector agreed, and the vast project began. Months went by, till at last over six hundred yards of barbed wire more than eight feet high surrounded the property, making it look like a prison camp from within, and from the outside a house prepared for seige.

The few people continuing to attend Densham's services remained unresponsive. This led to the second crucial incident. He hit upon an extraordinary device to lift the spirits of his congregation; he painted the Church red, yellow and blue, such deep hues as were used in medieval church decoration. In that strange innocence so typical of him, he did the work in secret, preferring not to consult the Church Council. He wanted to spring a surprise on his people.

We can imagine him there at the porch that first Sunday after his labours, words of welcome ready on his tongue, while he glanced back several times no doubt toward the predominantly red glow of the interior — then proudly leading his congregation. They were dumb-struck, probably standing stock still long enough for the consternation and horror on their faces to sink well into Densham's mind. Then murmuring began. It grew to a muttering till some self-appointed spokesman told Densham he had desecrated the House of The Lord, and walked out, followed by the others.

Things came to a head in 1933 when the parishioners of Warleggan petitioned the Bishop, Dr Walter Frere, to remove Densham. Studying their complaints, the Bishop elected to meet congregation and priest together, in their parish Church, a course of action hitherto unknown in Cornwall.

One evening then, Warleggan Church filled — for the last time in Densham's life — and now the congregation was a court. Light was requested. Densham complying, soon returned, bearing one candle. A solitary candle for so huge a gathering? To some such oddity illuminated, if little else, his impractical unworldly ways; to others, simply his witlessness.

The complaints against Densham took five different shapes. First, his critics complained, he had closed the Sunday School. Secondly, he had refused to hold services at convenient times.

Thirdly, he had converted Church property to his own use. Fourthly, he had threatened to sell the Church organ, a 1914-18 war memorial. And fifthly that he had erected a barbed wire fence inside the grounds of the Rectory.

Densham, however, told the Bishop that he was under no obligation to open the Sunday School, and that the reason for building the barricade around the Rectory grounds was to stop his dogs from worrying the farmers' sheep. Then came a sensation when the secretary of the Church Council alleged that the Rector had written to him threatening to kill him when he, the secretary, had prevented him from tearing up the Church. The Rector, however, told the inquiry that the secretary was mistaken — and the incident closed with the two men shaking hands.

The vituperation of Densham's accusers surprised the Bishop, but he determined on reconciliation, averring that the Rector had faithfully and constantly fulfilled his duties of office. He had never omitted to say services every Sunday. Therefore by ecclesiastical law he could not be removed. Emphasising Densham's loyalty to office, Dr Frere enjoined all to a fresh start.

And in a way that occasion did herald a fresh start, a new turning in the sad tale of the Reverend F.W. Densham. For that night the parishioners left Warleggan Church never to return, while for Densham began more or less two decades of silence ending in death.

What lay at the heart of parochial resentment as expressed that night was the Rector's authoritarian manner. For innocent though he was in day to day dealings, as a cleric he was authoritarian and this angered them. For centuries almost every acre of Warleggan, apart from glebe, had been owned by three squires. They and the Church had ruled the parish. In the thirties, however, the great estates were broken up by death duties; tenants bought their land, and for the first time were free to choose whom they did or did not respect. Church attendance ceased to be obligatory. Congregations began to diminish all over Cornwall. It was only in Warleggan where transition to a new order became a conflict; and a recalcitrant old-fashioned clergyman was broken by social change.

After the Bishop's visit that high fence around the Rectory suddenly changed in significance. It had been erected to keep in his dogs; now its purpose was to keep out people. The barbed wire at the gate was raised to twelve feet and then the unprofitable workmen were dismissed. Bitterness grew in his heart. Rejected, he rejected.

Now any workmen or caller arriving had to bang a petrol drum at the gate. Dogs would then charge down the drive followed slowly by the Rector calling upon the visitor to shout out his name and his business. Only then would he approach and unbar the gate. If the arrival was a workman hired to do a particular job, Densham would keep an eye on him all the time to see nothing was stolen. Sometimes when wages were paid, a workman would be told to look out of the window while the money was counted.

Densham became more and more, in the true sense of the word, eccentric. His life revolved not around the parish community but around his own increasingly bizarre world at the Rectory. However, for all his oddities, Densham had his supporters. One clergyman not far away recalls the Rector as 'no clown. I remember him coming to visit us; a thick, solid man . . . cheerful and bright . . . a bit odd perhaps, but then a lot of the Cornish clergy, in those days, *were* odd. They said if you stayed in Cornwall long enough, you went that way! There was something childlike about him. Yet, at the same time, he was a very sincere man. There was a spirituality about him that I don't think the Cornish people saw or understood.'

Of his quarrel with the Warleggan people, Densham once said, 'Before I came there was a daily Mass. I cut it out because it was illegal . . . and the Mass people stayed away. Then I refused to allow dancing and whist drives and the amusement lovers left.'

Gradually Densham became a near hermit. He avoided his parishioners, but welcomed visitors, provided they wrote and made an appointment. Once a fortnight a Bodmin grocery roundsman delivered a supply of oats, cheese, butter and margarine, leaving them in a box, just inside the entrance of the Rectory grounds. Densham relied on a daily diet of one meal, with porridge as his main course. He never consumed meat or fish or poultry or flesh of any kind.

One man who remembers the Rector well is Harry Willcock of Cardinham, the son of Herbert Willcock, sometime church warden at Warleggan and a loyal Densham ally. 'My father,' he recalls, 'would hear no bad against the Rector.'

However Harry, himself, reveals a few quirks in the man's make-

◀ Warleggan Rectory: 'Densham became more and more, in the true sense of the word, eccentric.'

up. 'He hated being watched. "Get on with your work," he'd say. He was also a stickler for time. He'd be waiting at the gate at five to eight in the morning, and if you were a few minutes late you'd have to hammer on the petrol drum and shout that you'd arrived. He could be a mistrustful man. If you were putting nails into something, he'd count how many you used. I used to post his letters, and he'd watch me from the kissing gate . . . I'd have to put one letter in the box at a time . . . and he'd count to make sure.'

Densham had a complex about hygiene. For example, he preferred rain water to well water. There could be an explosive side too. Harry Willcock recalls carving his initials on a door. 'The old man played Hell, and threatened that I should have to pay for a new door!

'There were certain things he didn't like, and one of them was smoking. When I came home on leave, and he saw me smoking, he asked, "Do they let you do that in the Army?" I replied, "Yes, they give us ten minutes in every hour for smoking." Densham was disgusted and walked away.'

It was now wartime. The downstairs windows were protected with sandbags, a look-out post and a fire escape were constructed, a multitude of catches were screwed in a row upon windows, three bolts were fitted on the front door, while on bedroom doors bolts were set not on the inside but the outside. Densham was shutting himself in. It was apparently the German invasion he feared but partly too that of his parishioners. Meanwhile outside the house natural activity furthered his aim. The great rhododendrons spread new growth and linked branches across the drive so no vehicle could enter. The laurels bordering the road grew so high that they blotted out all view of the parish.

The Rectory roof leaked apace. Ceilings cracked and fell. Throughout the house damp and decay took over the echoing rooms. Densham wrote to the District Council complaining that rates of £50 per annum were excessive for a house in such dilapidation. He complained that repairs were so costly that they, with such rates on top, left him scarcely any money for food out of his income of £265 per annum. The reply he received was a suggestion that as rates are based on rentable value he should advertise for tenants to take over some rooms. When, however, applicants saw the Rectory, its lack of electric light, of running water, of any amenity, none stayed.

Perhaps this attempt to find tenants suggested to Densham the idea of getting an organist to live at the Rectory. He was prepared to pay someone to live with him. He wrote to a choir school in the Midlands, stating that he had a vacancy at his church for an organist, who would live at the Rectory and play at Church services. A young man came and one can readily imagine the effect that remote Warleggan, the desolate Rectory within its jungled grounds, and the bedraggled old man had upon him. He stayed one night only. Densham was in the habit of locking bedroom doors at night and it was probably the sound of the bolt being pushed on the outside that most unnerved the organist. That room, in which no one had slept for many years, saw little sleep that night either. It was almost as though the Rector was prepared temporarily to imprison the organist in order to have company. No doubt, the young man was also dumbfounded to realise that not only would he have no choir to train but no congregation to play to. He left hurriedly the next morning.

After the disaster of the organist, Densham made yet another bid for companionship, and at accomplishing his pastoral trust. The Bishop, in that church scene long ago had suggested that he should concentrate his efforts upon the younger generation. If he won them over then their parents might think again about him. So Densham turned his attention to the children. He made prolonged efforts. He used to buy sweets in Bodmin and offer them to the children on his way home, but some mothers had warned their offspring not to accept anything from him. He did far more; part of the Rectory grounds still shows what he did. There, wrecked, but still recognisable, is the paraphernalia of an ambitiously constructed children's playground. You can see, amid leaves and brambles, the big cartwheel pivoted to serve as a merry-go-round, the rotted seat of a swing that hung between two trees, the cemented depression which was to be a boating pool, and the sandpit. A few evacuee children billeted nearby used the playground; no local child came near.

Densham also purchased a lantern slide projector and made blackout boards for the barn windows. Here he planned to give exciting shows. Fantastic Greek legends and stories from the Arabian Nights were to be shown. Some of his slides might be considered nightmarish — such as the portrayal of Polyphemus with his one eye gouged out; but Densham only thought such scenes would be extra thrilling for the youngsters. When the barn was ready, all apparatus set up, Densham announced the date of his first show. The time came. He waited expectantly in the dark — and once again his plans collapsed. No one came. What mother would allow her child to go into a dark room with the notorious Rector? His lantern slides still exist, in good condition. They include many that deal with 'health and hygiene in India'. Had he shown these to the children it is possible that in giving a commentary he would have unlocked the mystery of his past, describing perhaps a missionary life in India.

Evacuees from London were being billeted on sometimes unwilling households in the county. Densham informed the authorities responsible that he could accommodate many persons at his Rectory. He built cupboards and shelves, erected bunk beds and bought quantities of potatoes, which he stored carefully under mounds of earth. He purchased a large chip fryer.

The authorities visited his premises and were shown all that he had done. He mentioned too his magic lantern apparatus. A few days later he received a letter explaining that, as no woman was available to look after the children, the Rectory could not be considered.

After this, Densham accepted that there would be no one to whom he might minister. Yet he provided himself with companions of a sort: those members of the Church who were not now living on earth. He made out cards bearing the names of past Rectors of Warleggan, propped these cards around the Church pews and preached to them. These past Rectors became his closest and most real companions, sharing his suffering, for they in their time would have known, if not as greatly as he did, the coldness and rebuffs of their flock in this moorland parish, where, in a thousand years of Christian witness, fewer than half a dozen people had chosen to build their houses near the Church. In the presence of his predecessors Densham did not do all the preaching. They were surprised at times, no doubt, by a voice from a box, for Densham not only broadcast sermons to them but occasionally relayed the Brains Trust too. 'I am not sure that I do not prefer my congregation of ghosts,' he once confessed. 'They cannot object to any innovations I make.'

After his congregationless services, the Rector made the habit of locking up the Church and joining the Methodists in their nearby Chapel where he exhorted them to abstain 'from the Hellward follies of the world', which included such activities as reading a novel or going to the cinema or having a drink in a pub.

He was also occupied with another enterprise, that of transforming the Rectory into the Bible lands. You travelled from Cyprus or Alexandria across the landing to Pizgah where Moses first saw the Promised Land. Thence to Bethany, where Christ raised Lazarus from the tomb and to Emmaus where He Himself appeared after rising from the dead. Densham lived in his territory of spirits and sanctified the rooms by painting names and crosses on the doors. Small wonder that subsequent inhabitants should report that the house was haunted.

Down the years Densham chronicled his lonely services in the Church register. Under *Attendance* we see written 'No congregation at any services' over and over again right through the year even at Christmas. Occasionally he wrote 'Rectors cards put out'. Under *Remarks* he invariably included comments on the usually inclement weather. He wrote:

Warleggan Church: 'No rain, no wind, no sun, no congregation. . .'

'Severe gale with hail. Very cold' and 'No rain, no wind, no sun, no congregation. Both stoves burned excellently.'

In his last years one good parishioner did help him, lighting his stove and tending the garden. In the Church, the lettering in the register progressively charts the weakening hand. The records of his final annual parish Church meeting are similar to many previous ones:

> 3.15 p.m. Annual Parochial Church Meeting. Only the Rector attended; no quorum, waited until 3.40 p.m. No outstanding liabilities.

Holy Communion collection	NIL	
Per Boxes	1	0
For Church Account	11	3
Special Collections	NIL	
Total in respect of year	£- 12	2

On Christmas Day in 1952 no one attended the Church, as on all the Sundays of the year. The sermon was 'God is Love'.

In the New Year, however, he had an unexpected audience. A reporter and a photographer from *Life,* the American Weekly Journal and a reporter from *The Western Morning News* attended the service. Did he sense how the public who had shunned him were now to turn their curious gaze on him? The sermon 'On level headedness' is almost a cautionary warning to journalists not to distort the facts of his life.

Strangely, on the same day came another visitor too late for service. Densham records cryptically:

'At 3.10 came Tom Webster, British Railways.'

The following Sunday Warleggan Church held a large congregation and a good collection was taken — by a new Rector. Densham had died that week.

He had known how near death was. He placed on a table groups of apples with labels beside them, to be distributed to the sick of the parish. Then, this last act of charity accomplished, he went upstairs to die in bed. But he could not get there; three steps from the landing he collapsed, dead.

His body lay there for two days.

Now above the rhododendrons one chimney could be seen from the village. And from it in Densham's day smoke was ever wont to rise. When the villagers realised the fire was out they gonged the petrol drum at the gate, but there was no response. Now it would be an intrepid local indeed who would break through the fence, even when such ominous silence reigned. So the police were called and at last the defences were breached.

Some time before his death he had given instructions that his ashes should be scattered in the 'Garden of Remembrance'. This was his name for the plot of land ringed with laurels. His wishes were brushed aside. After his funeral attended by only one man — his solicitor — his body was cremated and the ashes scattered not in the land he had prepared but in another Garden of Remembrance, the official one in Plymouth.

One wish, however, was readily granted: that no memorial should mark his resting place.

Warleggan Church was thoroughly whitewashed, and the Rectory sold. There has never been another resident Rector of Warleggan. Shortly after his death, his possessions were auctioned, an event which drew a huge crowd of the curious to the Rectory. But no personal mementoes to give a clue to his life were under the hammer. A brother had arrived beforehand and Densham's papers, including several hundred files had been burnt. In the pigeon holes covering every wall of his study the Rector had kept a vast collection of items, storing information and thoughts there, parochial, theological and philosophical.

A page of jokes and some lecture notes, taken or given at Oxford in the last century were blowing round the cellar when I took over the house. A more baffling clue to the still mysterious Rector can scarcely be imagined.

Ghosts

I have never had the luck to meet a ghost. But then can I be sure? Would I have recognised 'it' as a ghost? Conversations with people who have seen an apparition have taught me one thing: some only realize later that they had actually seen a ghost.

Lovely, wooded St Nectan's Glen, roughly half-way between Tintagel and Boscastle, has produced many fascinating claims of ghostly sightings, and one of the first I heard, when coming to live at Bossiney in 1965, was from Mary Bowley, then a regular visitor to North Cornwall. She told me of an Army officer, on leave: his first visit to Cornwall, his first day down here, he decided to take a stroll up the glen before dinner. Over dinner, he remarked, 'By the way, I didn't know you had a monastery here.'

'A monastery?' someone countered curiously.

'Why, yes, I met three monks in the glen . . . all cheerful fellows!'

He had to be convinced he had seen three ghosts — and later admitted he knew nothing about the haunted reputation of the Glen with its monk-like figures. So but for that dinner-table conversation, he might have gone through the rest of his life, not knowing he had seen as many as three ghosts.

Perhaps we have to go to children's fiction to get some kind of explanation, to Roland Quizz's *Giant Land* and that telling piece of conversation:

> *'Gracious!' exclaimed Mrs Snip, 'and is there a place where people venture to live above ground?'*
>
> *'I never heard of people living under ground,' replied Tim, 'before I came to Giant Land.'*
>
> *'Came to Giant Land!' cried Mrs Snip, 'why, isn't everywhere Giant Land?'*

The fact is the vague, indistinct figure — the ghostly form in many minds — is often not the case. Peter Underwood in his comprehensive *Dictionary of the Occult & Supernatural* in the section devoted to ghosts writes 'Most witnesses agree that the spontaneous ghost of fact is not the wispy, transparent, ethereal figure of fiction but apparently substantial and three-dimensional.'

It is only when the figure vanishes inexplicably — say through a solid wall or a locked door — that realization may strike, and the truth dawns.

Despite the thousands of sightings, ghosts remain a mystery. What are they? Why do they appear?

Judy Chard, in her excellent *Devon Mysteries*, thought 'I don't think hauntings just occur — I think some particular physical presence is needed to cause an apparition to appear. Maybe there are people who attract the past in some way so that exorcism, if it is practised, has its effect on the people at the place and not on the supposed spirits. As a water diviner I know everything has its "field" or aura, so perhaps evil or good can impress itself and cause

St Nectan's Glen: '. . . has produced many claims of ghostly sightings.'

Lizard coastline: '. . . this cruel but beautiful coastline has been the graveyard of many ships.'

this atmosphere that many people feel. Some buildings seems to oppress us with a sense of the people who have lived and died in them. It isn't so very hard to understand, for the walls and floors and ceilings of old buildings must be saturated with the exhalations of human emotions. I read somewhere the theory that a shadow that once falls on a wall leaves a shadow there forever.'

I was reminded of Judy Chard's theory when I visited Pistol Meadow at the Lizard. Pistol Meadow is a grim reminder of the fact that this cruel but beautiful coastline of ours has been the graveyard of many ships and sailors. Back in the 1700s a transport ship, carrying seven hundred men, was wrecked off the Maenheere Rocks — with horrific loss of life — there were only two survivors. The victims were buried here in Pistol Meadow in mass graves.

Cornish-born author and theatre critic J.C. Trewin reflected: 'I can believe anything of this meadow especially after a December sunset. It was in December that I had an odd experience, about four o'clock on a calm, dull afternoon during the Armistice Autumn. In the narrows of the cliff path above Pistol, I heard someone coming, a brisk patter of feet and stood aside to let him pass. He was, as I remember, a shrivelled man in a nondescript blue guernsey, badly torn at the collar. He had a fuzz of wiry, greying hair. Nothing else was noticeable but his eyes, deep black in the extreme pallor of his face. I said, "Good afternoon." He brushed by me, without answering. A few seconds later, not more, I heard steps again, and there, coming towards me, was without a doubt the same man, though manifestly he could not have doubled round in so short a time and on so awkward a path. I stopped, more perplexed than frightened, and again said "Good afternoon." Again there was no reply. And then a third time, I heard steps. Now nothing was in sight. I felt a quick stirring in the air, but no-one passed me. Fear came, and I tore home through the darkening day.'

It was a very different day when I went to Pistol Meadow: a brilliantly sunlit July morning with the sea lying like satin beneath a light blue sky. Yachts sailed by: an idyllic scene. Yet in this silent green meadow, still damp with early morning dew, you felt a sombre something. The most interesting thing of all was the behaviour of my usually placid Collie Cross. That morning he had a nervous, agitated air, and I was reminded how a terrier had once behaved strangely on Rough Tor. Do animals have psychic feelings? I have long thought so, and as we walked up the lane from Pistol Meadow and Rex became his calmer self again, I felt a kind of confirmation in my bones.

Supernatural sounds, I have discovered, are far rarer than sightings. However some extremely interesting evidence has come to me through fellow Bossiney author Joan Rendell of Tremarsh, Launceston.

'I took my car to Truscotts in Launceston to be MOT'd,' she told me. 'The garage is on the site of the old Launceston Railway Station and while I was waiting for the car to be tested I took Zeus, my dog, for a walk along the old railway line in the Egloskerry direction. We walked for about half a mile before turning back towards Launceston when I *distinctly* heard a train coming behind us from the direction of Egloskerry. It was so real that I instinctively pulled Zeus on to the grass verge and stood looking back along the line, fully expecting to see a train come round the bend even though all the rails have gone. The sound lasted for fully a minute and was so eerie that it, as we say in Cornwall, "gave me quite a turn". I put it down to "wishful thinking" on my part as I loved that old railway and we were near the still remaining portion of the platform where, during my lifetime, I had experienced many happy moments, and many sad and emotional ones, especially during wartime.

'The interesting thing is that, after this experience, a friend from Launceston called bringing with him a friend of his from Liskeard who wanted an autographed copy of my book *Hawker Country*. The Liskeard man is a railway "buff" so after they left here they went to Tresmeer and Otterham to have a look at the remains of the stations there and take some photographs.

'A few evenings later John, my Launceston friend, rang to say how they had both enjoyed *Hawker Country*, and I asked them how they had got on when visiting the old North Cornwall stations. He shook me rigid because he said, "You know where the curve is by the arch at Tresmeer, well, we'd just walked along there and were talking about the railway when we both stopped and looked round, and I said to Doug 'Do you hear what I hear?' and he said 'If there were still rails here I could swear a train was coming'." They had heard exactly the same thing as I had heard and they are both "down to earth" sort of men who are not, as far as I know, in the least bit psychic. I then told John of my experience and he was flabbergasted. I'd not have told anyone if he had not related his experience first. To me it had been all so vivid . . . I was sure that train was coming round by Town Mills.'

No Body — Strange Death of Cornish Author

Of all the authors who people the Cornish literary scene, Crosbie Garstin is the one I would most like to have met.

Apart from the brilliance of his writing — personally, I put his trilogy, *The Owl's House, High Noon* and *The West Wind,* in the top bracket of Cornish novels — he had a larger than life quality. He of the great departed troop of authors is the one I would have loved to interview or, better still, get to know and yet, in a way, we meet every day. His photograph stands in my office: a lean figure in a polo-necked sweater sitting against a boat at Lamorna. Lantern-jawed, dark hair neatly parted, a moustached man of action relaxing: a character who might have stepped from the pages of a Hemingway novel or short story. Indeed parts of his life read like chunks of fiction, and his death, tragically early at the age of 43, remains cloaked in mystery.

He was born in Penzance — not Newlyn as has so often been said — in a house in Alexandra Road, near the Pirates' Rugby ground, something he would have liked for he had a passion for the game, so much so that at the age of fifteen he wrote:

I envy not the King his crown
  The Earl his coronet
The Dean may keep his cap and gown,
  For such I do not fret
The Bishop can his mitre wear
  The Cardinal his hat
The poet may his laurels bear
  In fact the truth is that
For any of his set
  I do not care a rap.
But oh! I'd give my head to get
  An Irish Rugby Cap!

His father was Norman Garstin, an Irishman, a painter and pioneer in creating Newlyn as an artists' colony. There were three children: a second son Denis who was killed in action in Russia in 1918, and a sister Alethea, well known in her own right as a painter.

At her home high above St Ives on that beautiful corkscrewing coastal road at Zennor, near D.H. Lawrence's cottage, we talked about her brother Crosbie as a boy. At school he resembled Sir Winston Churchill in that he rarely shone in examinations, his headmaster describing him as 'one of the laziest boys I have ever taught but the only genius my school has produced'.

His career got off to all kinds of false starts, and eventually his parents despatched him to Canada to work on a ranch belonging to friends. In Canada he did a variety of jobs: a bronco buster, breaking wild horses; a sawyer in the lumber camps; a miner on the Pacific coast; a member of a threshing gang — and even a chucker-out. But the poet in him was beginning to mature and poetry written in Canada was later to appear in his first book *Vagabond Verses*.

After Canada he went to Bechuanaland to manage a ranch. 'His arrival there,' Alethea Garstin told me, 'coincided with the worst drought for years. It was so bad that he had to keep a pebble between his lips, and because there was no water he had to shoot the cattle himself.' Surviving the drought, he also became ranger to the Tati Concession which made him a kind of one-man police force. In Europe, however, the storm clouds of war were gathering and he returned to England to enlist as a ranker in the King Edward's Horse, a crack Colonials force. A year later he was commissioned in the field. On the Western Front he experienced Flanders, with all its mud and misery and despite it all the poet inside the uniform continued to flower.

His first book, *Vagabond Verses*, was published in 1917, and by now his prose was getting published in magazine form, much of which later appeared in a book entitled *The Mudlarks*, an amusing collection of essays put together at the front.

When the war was over, he concentrated on writing, producing a dozen books — one in conjunction with Mrs Alfred Sedgwick — and

◀ Author Crosbie Garstin: 'his body was never found — we shall never know the full story.'

a whole host of articles and short stories.

But in retrospect Crosbie Garstin's reputation rests firmly on the Penhale trilogy. First came *The Owl's House* — I never enter the Angel Hotel at Helston without thinking of that brilliant opening chapter, John Penhale with his badly scarred face to the wall — then *High Noon*, and finally *The West Wind*. The irony of this trilogy is that he set out to write only a single novel. In the original manuscript of *The Owl's House*, Penhale dies in the last chapter. But his publisher Heinemann telegrammed: 'Re-write last chapter. Penhale too good a character to kill off!'

At night I have travelled from Helston to Penzance and have tried to recreate John Penhale's ride by horse on that same but different road. 'In imagination he saw the Squire's daughter as he was always seeing her on dark nights when he was alone, strucken numb in his arms, glazed horror in her eyes — saw her running across the blind country, sobbing, panting, stumbling in the furrows, torn by brambles, trying to get home away from him, the terror. He shut his eyes, as though to shut out the vision, and rode on past Germoe to Kenneggy Downs.

'The moon was flying through clouds like a circus-girl through hoops; the road was swept by winged shadows. Puddles seemed to brim with milk at one moment, ink the next. At one moment the surrounding countryside was visible, agleam with hoar frost, and then blotted out in darkness; it was a night of complete and startling transformations. The shadow of a bare oak leapt upon them suddenly, flinging unsubstantial arms at man and horse as though to grasp them a phantom octopus. Penhale's mare shied, nearly unseating him. He came out of his sombre thoughts, kicked spurs into her, and drove her on at a smart trot. She swung forward trembling and uneasy, nostrils swelling, ears twitching, as though she sensed uncanny presences abroad.'

I have recently been dipping into the Garstin novels again after a gap of seven years. Once more I found myself hurrying from paragraph to paragraph, eager to turn the page, halting now and then reflecting on the quality of his authorship, of the magic — for me — he still weaves.

At 43, of course, he had not yet reached his Everest. With average luck, more books and greater fame must surely have lain ahead of him. Like the great Cornish painter Peter Lanyon, in more recent times, one is struck by the sheer waste.

That perceptive poet of Penwith, Arthur Caddick, wrote of Peter Lanyon, dying at roughly the same age:

> He filled his meagre years with work, kept faith
> With talent. He made glowing pigments of his own,
> His mind all adamant to understand
> The core of things direct not secondhand.

Such words might apply to Crosbie Garstin. One brought Life with paint, the other with words: both original.

And what about the man behind the books?

I feel that I know at least a few of the pieces in the jig-saw puzzle of his personality. I say jig-saw puzzle because there were seemingly contradictions. Peggy Garside, a neighbour and good friend in our Bossiney days, remembered him as 'a brilliant swimmer . . . father would say "If Crosbie's in the swimming party, I know you'll be safe," ' and yet incredibly the man died through drowning. He loved his father, but they argued for hours. He was an excellent marksman but hated killing anything. Charles Simpson, the painter, rated him 'a marvellous raconteur', but his wife Ruth remembered him for the fact that 'he held up every dinner party with his story-telling' — an opinion readily endorsed by his sister Alethea: 'Crosbie never ate a hot meal in his life!' Rex Carr, Headmaster for many years at St Erbyn's, Penzance, recalls him as Guest of Honour at the school's first sports and speech day making a speech 'full of good sense and humour'. Another contemporary called him 'The life and soul of any group, but once he was in full flow you couldn't get a word in edgeways.'

Even his marriage to Lilian can read like something out of a novel: two girls holidaying at Lamorna, one gets into difficulties swimming and is rescued by Crosbie. The other girl, in gratitude, flings her arms around him, and within a matter of weeks they are engaged.

His death or mysterious disappearance is a true Westcountry mystery, to be precise a Devonshire mystery, for it happened at Salcombe, that pretty village, sheltered within the estuary on the South Devon coast.

It was a sailing invitation to join the Holman family that led to the tragedy. Miss Olive Wesley, who typed many of his manuscripts and ran a typing school in South Parade, Penzance, told me that he insisted on getting his novel typed and away to the publishers before finally accepting the invitation: 'He was working at tremendous pressure to finish *The West Wind*,' she recalled, 'and in a strange sort of way I blame myself for his death in that I typed into the early hours of the morning so that the novel could be sent to London.'

Typing finished, and manuscript posted, Garstin, joined the Holmans on their yacht. At Salcombe, on this first night, however, he felt tired and said he would not join the others who were going ashore to a party. Later in the evening he became bored, changed his mind and came ashore. And much later in the evening he and a young lady in a fur coat, together with another person, set out for the yacht in a pram — a small boat that normally carries only two passengers. A short distance from the shore, in total darkness, the pram began to sink, the third member of the party swam back to shore for help, while the young lady later admitted that she owed her life to the fact that 'invisible hands' removed her fur coat and helped her to get back to land. In the process of saving her life, Crosbie Garstin lost his own. Drama and mystery deepened in that his body was never found.

The curious thread which sometimes links fact and fiction can be found in the penultimate chapter of *The West Wind* with Ortho Penhale preferring death to capture: 'the boom of the surf was the deep roll of drums. The wind blew with the sound of trumpets, piercing, exultant. The phantom clippers dipped their gilded beaks, most stately, the ghostly soldiers tossed their lances, 'Come on, old comrade,' they cried. 'Fear not! Death is but a pang and life immortal. Ride on with us, ride on forever!'

'A roller surged over the rock ledges, up and up, wrapping white foam about Ortho's knees; spume flakes spattered his bare chest, flecked his black bull curls. He flung both hands towards the rising sun saluted — and plunged.'

Strange prophetic words.

And some sixteen pages later in the Epilogue came his last published paragraph: 'Anthony Penhale sat motionless for a long while in thought. Then rising, he kissed the happy face and went downstairs to tell his wife that all was over — or all beginning.'

Was it all over? Or was there another beginning?

And I am not thinking of any theological explanation — that death is not the end but merely a door opening.

At the time of the incident, some people did think that Crosbie

Garstin had vanished into thin air — to make a new start elsewhere. Unlike Lord Lucan, he was no wanted man. The suggestion was that he simply wanted to start again — and with his undoubted wanderlust that must have been a possibility. He and Lilian had been married only four years, and one of those he had spent travelling around the world, writing for a magazine.

Others, the majority it is fair to say, believe it was just a tragic death, a deep, dark tragedy. But the fact remains his body was never found — consequently we shall never know the full story.

Acknowledgments

Recently I was back in front of those Chapel windows at Bossiney. It struck me as a good place to end an excursion among some of the Cornish mysteries. After all, but for those strange lights in 1965 I should not be here where I am today: at the end of a third exploration, and running a publishing business with Sonia in the Cornish countryside.

Once more, I am indebted to the people, who gave me interviews, or allowed me to quote them. Their thoughts and particularly those, who have shared experiences that test logic, all combine to remind us that Cornwall is an exciting place in which to live and work. Cornwall is both a privilege and a challenge.

Finally, my special thanks to the small Bossiney team. Apart from the various photographers, I am grateful to Brenda Duxbury, who has edited this and all our Bossiney titles, Janet Down who has typed the greater part of it, and my wife Sonia who has been about other Bossiney business while I have explored these fascinating themes.

ALSO AVAILABLE

GHOSTS OF CORNWALL
by Peter Underwood
Peter Underwood, President of the Ghost Club, journeys across haunted Cornwall. Photographs of haunted sites and drawings of ghostly characters all combine to prove that Cornwall is indeed a mystic land.
'Britain's top ghost-hunter . . . fascinating . . .'
The Sunday Independent

GHOSTS OF DEVON
by Peter Underwood
Peter Underwood, President of the Ghost Club, writes of ghostly stories that saturate the county of Devon, a land full of mystery and of ghostly lore and legend.
'Packed with photographs, this is a fascinating book.'
Herald Express

GHOSTS OF SOMERSET
by Peter Underwood
The President of the Ghost Club completes a hat-trick of hauntings for Bossiney.
'. . . ghostly encounters that together make up the rich tapestry of the Ghosts of Somerset.'
Western Gazette

WESTCOUNTRY HAUNTINGS
by Peter Underwood
'The Westcountry offers . . . just about every kind of ghostly manifestation . . .' writes Peter Underwood, President of the Ghost Club. *'. . . a chilling look at hauntings from Bristol to Cornwall . . . many of the accounts appear for the first time.'*
David Henderson, The Cornish Guardian

E.V. THOMPSON'S WESTCOUNTRY
This is a memorable journey: combination of colour and black-and-white photography. Bristol to Land's End happens to be the Bossiney region, and this is precisely E.V. Thompson's Westcountry.
'Stunning photographs and fascinating facts make this an ideal book for South West tourists and residents alike — beautifully atmospheric colour shots make browsing through the pages a real delight.'
Jane Leigh, Express & Echo